CONFESSIONS OF A CPA: THE TRUTH ABOUT LIFE INSURANCE

BY

Bryan S. Bloom, CPA

Copyright © 2013 by Bryan S. Bloom, CPA

ISBN 978-0-7414-9976-9

Printed in the United States of America

Published December 2013

INFINITY PUBLISHING
1094 New DeHaven Street, Suite 100
West Conshohocken, PA 19428-2713
Toll-free (877) BUY BOOK
Local Phone (610) 941-9999
Fax (610) 941-9959
Info@buybooksontheweb.com
www.buybooksontheweb.com

What others are saying about Confessions of a CPA: Why What I Was Taught To Be True Has Turned Out Not To Be

Eye Opening! Great read.
Great book and very eye-opening. I would highly recommend to anyone who is tired of listening to conventional wisdom. Written at a very easy-to-understand level.
Larry

Finally! The Truth About Money!
I have been looking for this book for a long time. As a CPA, I have seen over and over again that money does not work the way conventional wisdom promises. To make matters worse, I was at a loss for an alternative process. Confessions of a CPA is written in plain English and explains everything you never thought about regarding the movement of money - complete with tax consequences.
B.A.

This is "New Wine" for Hungry People.
Confessions of a CPA is unique in that the author's background enables him to "prove" the arguments - not just make the arguments - and explain WHY these "truths" aren't working out very well. We all know that something hasn't been right with the establishment line. Now it makes sense.
Alan

Confessions of a CPA is one of the best books on finance that I have read. I wish I had read it 30 years ago. It is practical and easily read. I am changing some of my long-term planning as a result of reading this book.
Bob S.

The Truth Will Set You Free!
Confessions of a CPA cuts through the clutter, the half-truths and the misinformation that has been taught to the financial industry and preached to the public. Confessions address the inaccuracies of key financial concepts that have dramatic effects on our financial futures. The author clearly explains

and documents the truth about how money "REALLY" works! This information is crucial for all professionals in the financial services industry as well as any individual who is serious about their financial future. It is only the truth that you know that will set you free!
Ron L

Confessions of a CPA is one of the best and most concise books that I have ever read on challenging the validity of some long-held financial beliefs.
Jim D.

Finally.
I am so glad that someone has taken the time to write a book on how money really works. Everyone gets hung up on rates of return and all we are really told is the average rate of return, not the actual. The truth is money is not math and math is not money.
Jason

Confessions of a CPA is a good read. Intelligent financial planning, investment insights and sprightly written.
Fred

Wonderful!
Confessions of a CPA was a book that needed to be written. It sheds light on why common financial planning fails to meet expectations and how it takes some thinking outside of the box to get uncommon results.
Jeremy P

Myths of Traditional Financial Planning Dispelled.
Confessions of a CPA is a quick read and should be required background reading for anyone working with a financial planner/advisor. It will give you the ammunition you need to ask the right questions and the tough questions. I am a CPA and learned a lot - I had been thinking about things the wrong way all these years.
M. Paul

Excellent Advice.
Creating wealth sounds extremely difficult, but the author breaks it down to a simplistic method to building a more secure approach to growing your wealth.
Ken

Break the Cycle.
I learned about the ever-depleting process of getting caught in our debt-based system. The book expounds on the why things are and how to escape the trap.
Osmo

Truth!!!!!!!!!!!!!!!!!!!!!!!!!!!!!!!!!!!
An honest CPA! <u>Confessions of a CPA</u> is an enormous help in determining just what is really important and what is not, financially speaking.
John Marrs

In Memory Of

Jeffry John Bloom

1958-2013

To my brother, whose love and support can never be replaced. Jeffry made financial preparation for his eventual retirement. Even though he would never see those retirement years, he used the principles of this book during his life which ultimately left a financial legacy to the ones he loved.

Acknowledgements

Writing a book is a challenging experience and it is not done alone! There are many people who make the words on a page both easily understandable and interesting for the reader.

This book could not have been written without the love and support of family.

First and foremost I am grateful to my Heavenly Father, the Yahweh of the Old Testament of the Bible, who lets me call him "Abba Father," and His Son, Jesus Christ, who is my personal Lord and Savior.

My earthly family has been indispensable to my process of writing this book. I am thankful for the encouragement of my spouse of 32 years; Pam lifts me to heights of excellence and integrity not achievable on my own. I am grateful for her inspiration every day. Our two daughters have participated in bringing this book from concept to reality. Callie Sederquist has been indispensable as a financial professional in her own right. Her knowledge of financial products has expanded my own understanding. Corrie Musgrave did a wonderful job helping me to word sections of the book just right. She served as my consistency editor. She helped me by editing to ensure congruency between the charts and chart discussions. She was also influential in helping me envision Confessions of a CPA as a potential series of books, not just Confessions of a CPA II.

My extended family was vital. The way you verbally say something isn't necessarily how you write something. But that is what I did. Jeff and Abby Abbott were my frontline editors. I think it took longer to edit the book than it did to write it. They did a great job. They also served the purpose of being you, my target audience. They read the manuscript from your perspective and helped me to bring clarity to portions that were difficult to understand.

Soon after the publishing of my original Confessions of a CPA book, I was asked if there was going to be a sequel. There have been two sequels to Confessions of a CPA - Why What I Was Taught To Be True Has Turned Out Not To Be. Those two books took the principles of the original book and repackaged them in terms that those in the practice of medicine would find helpful. My good friend, Sean Quigley helped bring Dental Wealth and Life$cience to the marketplace. Sean and I work closely with clients and I appreciate his positive outlook on life.

I am often asked to train other financial professionals using the content of my books. Rob McPheters has provided me with ample opportunities to train financial professionals in the application of the principles of this book.

In my hometown of Champaign, Illinois, I get to rub shoulders with some of the best in the financial arena. Central Illinois is blessed to have people like Jamie Chesser, John Butler, Jim Lilley, Terri Wetzel, Jason Fagan, Tim Noice and Scott Olthoff to consult with. I see them every day. As Proverbs 27:17 says: "iron sharpens iron, so one person sharpens another." So true!

Lastly, I want to thank you, the reader of Confessions of a CPA. You are not only reading the book, but you are putting it into practice. I have heard story after story of how the principles in these books have helped you. That is the real motivation in my writing. If I can make a difference in another family's life with the lessons I have personally learned, then the effort that goes into writing is worthwhile. Thank you.

Forward

Helping people establish sound financial foundations is often challenging for a financial advisor.

Financial regulations seem to change daily, creating misunderstanding and frequently uncertainty for clients. These changes make it important and necessary for proper discloser, yet can add confusion to the person seeking advice. Regulations and disclosures are essential, but shouldn't be so overbearing causing clients and advisors to be stymied with frustration, and just do nothing.

Even more problematic in our society is widespread miscommunication concerning financial security. Daily a person can read or hear conflicting financial recommendations and question whether to participate in the company's 401(k) plan, or reduce taxes now and pay them later, or pay them now so taxes aren't due in the future.

In addition, there is much confusion regarding how life insurance plays a part of a person's Financial Plan. I'm asked often, "Should I own term or permanent insurance?" As Bryan points out is this book, the answer is YES! In each of our lifetimes, there is a time and a place for both.

In this sequel to his book, <u>Confessions of a CPA – Why What I Was Taught to be True Has Turned Out Not to Be</u>, Bryan hits the nail on the head with this new "Confessions of a CPA" book. In <u>The Truth About Life Insurance,</u> Bryan accurately unlocks the mysteries of life insurance basics and innovatively depicts how life insurance works in a strong Financial Plan.

I learned a long time ago, that the most expensive thing a person can own is a *closed mind.*

Personally, I like Bryan's approach precisely explaining the Living benefits of life insurance. We all know life insurance was designed to provide financial protection in knowing a death benefit will be available to assure the hopes and dreams a young couple has starting out in life, will be seen to completion, even if one passes away prematurely. But what Bryan discloses in the second half of the book is how the presence of that death benefit during life unleashes the power of every other financial asset we own.

I appreciate the integrity Bryan approaches life with. Besides being friends and colleagues we share a common bond. We were the first two recipients of the Chairman's Navigator Award awarded by one of the country's most stable life insurance companies. The Chairman's Navigator Award first awarded in 2008 "salutes a sales associate who exhibits the highest standard of professionalism, dedication, commitment and leadership … and who is of exceptional integrity and character. The Chairman's Navigator award symbolizes the ongoing commitment to 'finding a way forward.'"

This book, <u>Confessions of a CPA – The Truth About Life Insurance</u>, tries to find a way forward. It embraces the spirit of the Navigator Award. It reveals not only truth, but Bryan's heart that life insurance plays a vital part in every successful financial plan.

Michael Kinzie
Chartered Financial Consultant
Cincinnati, Ohio

Important Disclosures

This book contains a discussion of investments in general and life insurance in detail.

Whether illustrating investment returns or life insurance cash value, hypothetical illustrations (as contained in this book) may not be relied on as a certain prediction of or projection of those results.

Since life insurance is discussed extensively in this book:

Tax-free withdrawals and loans assume that the life insurance policy is properly funded and is not a modified endowment contract. Withdrawals are generally treated first as tax-free recovery of basis and then as taxable income, assuming the policy is not a modified endowment contract. However, different rules generally apply in the first fifteen policy years, when distributions accompanied by benefit reductions may be taxable prior to basis recovery. Loans from policies that are not classified as modified endowment contracts are generally not subject to tax but may be taxable if the policy lapses, is surrendered, exchanged or otherwise terminated. In the case of a modified endowment contract, loans and withdrawals are taxable to the extent of policy gain and a 10% penalty may apply if taken prior to age 591⁄2. Always confirm the status of a particular loan or withdrawal with a qualified tax advisor. Cash value accumulation may not be guaranteed depending on the type of product selected.

Income tax-free death benefits, withdrawals and loans apply to Federal taxes only. State income taxes may apply. Loans and withdrawals will reduce the death benefit.

It is important that you consult with your own qualified tax advisor regarding your particular situation.

Table of Contents

PART I – Life Insurance Basics

PART II – How Life Insurance Works

PART I

Life Insurance Basics

Chapter 1

Why Life Insurance?

Insurance is all around us. We insure our cars, our homes, our income, and our life. In fact, we even insure our appliances! Have you ever purchased an extended warranty on your refrigerator? In essence, you have purchased disability insurance on your appliance since an extended warranty is nothing more than a guarantee that the refrigerator will still work when it can't. You have insured it against a short-term disability. That ought to make you think about your own personal income disability insurance coverage, but that is a subject for another book.

———————

Principle #1:

Insurance is better to *have* and not need than to *need* and not have.

———————

The problem about insurance is that it is never a good financial investment unless you have to file a claim. But if you have to file a claim, that means something bad has happened, and you would really prefer not to have to file a claim.

Insurance is a product you hope to never use. But if you never use it, you have still paid for the policy, and therefore have wasted a lot of money.

Some insurance you have to purchase. If you own a home that is financed with a mortgage, one of the conditions of being granted the mortgage is that the finance company requires that your property be insured against loss. If you own a car, the state that you live in may require you to purchase liability insurance. This is so that if you are in an accident and you are at fault, the injured individuals have some way of being compensated for their loss. If you don't purchase this insurance; you can't legally drive.

Liability insurance to cover the unintended consequences of driving a car is really a good thing to own. Without it, all of your assets (that are not protected by the laws of the state you live in) as well as your income are subject to loss and confiscation in the event of your negligent driving.

Consider this: suppose you are driving home from the office or on your way to pick up the kids. The first moment you are distracted the light turns red and you don't see it. You collide with another car driven by someone who is injured as a result. Their injury results in medical bills and they are unable to work for a year. Who is going to pay for this loss? You are, unless you have an adequate level of liability insurance to cover such a situation. What if the table is turned and you are the injured party and, in fact, the accident has cost your life? How much would you want your family to sue the negligent party for? If the words, "as much as they can" crossed your mind, you are in the grand majority. In fact, you are *irreplaceable* to your family. "As much as they can" will only replace your potential earning power for the rest of your life. Some would call this your economic human life value. Turn the table again; if you are sued for "as much as they can," do you have adequate liability insurance?

What if your death is not the result of a tragic automobile accident? What if it is something like a heart attack – just as sudden, but something that is not the fault or liability of someone else? Will your economic human life value be replaced for your family? Who is going to write that check?

Sometimes death doesn't come suddenly, as in an automobile accident or sudden heart attack. Sometimes it comes slower and at a more predictable, yet earlier than anticipated rate. Cancer and diabetes can result in a shortened life expectancy. This can, in fact, be more devastating financially than a sudden death since a death benefit won't be payable until the death occurs (even though income stops and financial obligations pile up). If you don't *already* have life insurance, the illness will more than likely render you uninsurable. Thus, life insurance will no longer be an available option for you. Life insurance must be purchased when you don't need it. When you need it you can't have it. Again, when it comes to insurance, *it is better to have and not need than to need and not have*.

Principle #2:

If I want my "economic human life value" to be replaced after my death, I must act *before* it becomes a pressing need.

What is your economic human life value? The best determiner of your economic human life value is an entity experienced in making these kinds of calculations, such as a life insurance company. They are in the business of calculating risks and spreading the cost of those risks over a large number of people. There is a point of diminishing value where the amount of coverage is excessive and they just won't go beyond. That is your economic human life value. Some say it is 15-25 times your income, depending on your age. The U.S. federal government, in the wake of the 9/11 terrorist attacks on the United States, determined the economic human life values of those who lost their lives in the World Trade Center and the Pentagon. Those values ranged from a low of 12.5 times an income to a high of 32 times an income (CNN Money, September 7, 2011, "9/11 10 years later, The 9/11 Fund: Putting a Price on Life," http://money.cnn.com/2011/09/06/news/economy/911 comp ensation fund/index.htm). Do your own calculation. How much money would it take to replace you? A multiple of 20 times your income would require a steady 5% rate of return every year to replace your income (without any allowance for compensation increases or spending lump sums of the death proceeds). Yes, it is a staggering number, but it is what you are financially worth to your family!

Principle #3:

If it is ever my spouse's desire to remarry after my death, I want it to be out of love and not because of the need for money. *Life insurance gives them this option.*

In the event of your untimely death, how will your spouse make up for the loss of your economic human life value?

Some might say, "my spouse will remarry." Others may assume their spouse will get a job or a second job. Still others might think, "if I buy enough life insurance, my spouse will not have to work or remarry and even though my family will have to move ahead without me, it will be without financial hardship."

If you say, "my spouse will remarry," have you ever had that conversation with your spouse before it became your conclusion? If not, I suggest you do. If your spouse remarries, whom would you want for him or her? Would you like the second marriage to be for love or for the need of money? The decision to remarry or not is a lot easier when financial concern can be removed from the remarriage question. After all, the decision should come from the same perspective in which you married – for love!

———————

Principle #4:

If my spouse ever has to face the future without me (and my income), I don't want my death to change all of the other hopes and dreams we had together for our family. *Life insurance gives my family this option.*

———————

In the event of your untimely death, how would your family continue to live the life you and your spouse dreamt of together without the assistance of your economic human life value? If you say, "my spouse will get a job," have you ever considered why your spouse isn't working now? If it is for the consideration of child rearing, does the dream of mom or dad staying home with kids change just because someone has died? I would think not. During the period of dating and engagement, many dreams are constructed. After marriage, these dreams are begun and carried out over a lifetime. I don't want my spouse to work if they don't want to. I still want my children to go to college. And I want them to be able to go to the college of their choice rather than to have to settle for something more affordable that doesn't offer a quality curriculum.

Life insurance is a great way to insure that the dreams of our early years really do come true. Life insurance isn't a necessary evil, as some think — life insurance is a dream realizer.

Chapter 2

Temporary Life Insurance Basics

In this chapter, the life insurance that you are better having and perhaps not needing is called temporary or term life insurance. It is the type of life insurance that will replace your economic human life value if you should meet your untimely end during a specific, temporary period of time. It is better known as death insurance. The only way to collect is to die.

Term life insurance is good and necessary for making sure that your family will be provided for financially if you should die. It ensures that all of the hopes and dreams you have with and for your family will be achieved even if you are no longer there.

This type of life insurance can be purchased in various ways. It can be purchased with an annual premium amount that increases every year with age, or with a premium that stays level for a certain period of time and then increases with age after that period of time expires. At a certain point, the annual increases in cost are prohibitive, but that generally happens after the children are done with college and on their own - otherwise known as "off the family payroll!" At that time, it is just mom and dad in their retirement years without the "need" for life insurance. Therefore, when the cost gets too expensive, they just drop the life insurance policy and consider themselves "self-insured." They become "self-insured" because during the course of their lives they have accumulated a nest egg equal to the amount of term life insurance that just expired.

So what does term life insurance cost? Often thought of as the least expensive way to buy life insurance, it can actually be the most costly if you never file a claim.

The first step in calculating the cost of term life insurance is to first calculate how much death benefit you want. Thinking back to the 20 times income figure to calculate economic human life value, consider a wage earner earning $100,000 a year. This is a good amount to consider because it is easily scalable: if you earn $200,000 a year, just double the calculations (and so on).

If a spouse needed to replace $100,000 per year and he or she could earn a rate of return of 5% consistently and safely every year, a nest egg of $2,000,000 is necessary. Some would consider this nest egg the deceased's economic human life value, but it actually falls short when you account for what the future may hold. All that this amount really means is the family could continue to live at the same standard of living as they did without the need to generate the lost wage through trading the family's time for money. Now remember that this number is 20 times income and for many insurance companies that stretches the upper limits of what they will provide. This amount of death benefits ignores the likelihood of earning a 5% rate of return every year and the family need for periodic lump sums for things like cars, vacations, college educations, and weddings. If you add these variables to the mix, the deceased's economic human life value is better defined as: "as much as the insurance company is willing to provide."

Principle #5:

I ought to get as much life insurance coverage as I can get because there is not a large enough sum of money that *an insurance company will issue that can fund the future* that my family and I have dreamt of.

Term life insurance is often thought of as the least expensive way to purchase life insurance. However, when you account for all the costs - including the opportunity cost of never having the term insurance premiums in your investment accounts earning interest - it can, in fact, be the most costly life insurance.

Let's consider a hypothetical 25-year-old that is just married and starting a family while earning $100,000 per year. The hypothetical premium for a $2,000,000 life insurance contract is $385 per year for 10 years. This is a contract with a premium that stays level for ten years, where the insured individual is in the best of health, and with no additional bells and whistles (which will be discussed in Chapter 4). Pretty cheap!

Remember that the recommended minimum insurance for a 25-year-old with a $100,000 yearly income is $2,000,000. Also remember that that amount of temporary term insurance costs $385 per year for the first 10 years.

At age 35 the premium on this policy goes to $4,445 (not too cheap anymore), so he goes shopping for another ten-year-level premium payment term policy. This time around, his health has slipped a bit - a little cholesterol problem, but that's all - and his new $2,000,000 policy premium becomes $585, which is still considered cheap. But we begin to have a problem; $585 no longer covers his human life value any longer, because in those ten years between age 25 and 35 he has received a raise and is now earning $150,000. Now his human life value is $3,000,000 and the premium goes to $835. Now, if you are thinking, "they don't really need that much," you need to re-read Chapter 1! If this were you and your spouse passed away unexpectedly, what are you willing to cut out of your young family's lifestyle (which now includes not only your spouse, but three children ages 8, 5 and 2)?

Let's skip ahead 10 more years. You are now 45 years of age. You have one child entering college and two children in high school. Your income is now $200,000 and your term premium in year 11 is $14,065. Whoa – let's apply for another 10-year policy. The insurance company has now started to lower its multiple on you. Instead of providing 20 times your income, they will only provide 15 times your income. You are also at one more reduced health rating because you've become "too short" for the same health rating as before – meaning that your height hasn't kept up with your weight changes. All of this considered, the same $3,000,000 policy's new ten-year premium would be $2,875 per year. Ouch, we've gone from $835 to $2,875; and with your oldest child just entering college and two not far behind!

Let's go another decade down the road. Now you are 55 and you figure you must work to 65 because you have to replace all of that tuition you spent from your savings. It looks like you have one more 10-year time frame to cover! This time around, the multiplier is reduced to 10 times your income and we'll assume you have topped off your income at $200,000 per year. You have also dropped one more health rating since you now have added some negative family history to your personal health record. With these new considerations, you find yourself spending $5,985 per year for the next 10 years.

Moving to year 65. It is now the night before your official retirement dinner and you are alone with your spouse at your favorite restaurant. You look lovingly into your spouse's eyes and you begin to reminisce about all those years of working and raising a family. You tell them the financial plan has worked, all those years of paying for all that cheap term insurance has finally come to an end, and tomorrow you are going to cancel your policy. Today, your spouse would get $2,000,000 if you died, but tomorrow, because your plan was so successful, they would get $0. Assuming you make it through the night, the first question your spouse might ask the next morning is how much was spent to acquire all that insurance that you are cancelling today.

So let's add up all that cheap insurance: $385 per year for the first 10 years is $3,850; $835 per year for the second 10 years is $8,350; $2,875 per year for the third 10 is $28,750; and $5,985 for each of the last 10 years is $59,850. Together, that makes a grand total of $100,800. Your spouse is no dummy and knows that is only part of the cost. What you are not counting is what you otherwise could have earned on that money had you invested it. This is known as opportunity cost. Every dollar spent is a dollar that can never be saved, invested, earn interest, or be spent again, and neither can what it might have earned while in your possession. If, instead, you had invested this money over those 40 years in an account earning 7% , you discover that the true cost of that insurance was really $263,185. Your spouse's next question is whether this amount you have put in trust with the insurance company is going to be refunded to you since they never had to pay out the death benefit. The answer is no, this money is not going to be available for your use in retirement.

Thinking a little more on opportunity cost, let's assume you live another 20 years to full life expectancy (age 85). The initial $100,800 that you spent for your (now expired) term life insurance could have continued to grow at a rate of, say, 7%. At age 85, the money that could have been $263,185 when you were age 65 could now be $889,546! Surely that will be refunded to your children now that you have passed on. No - your insurance policy was cancelled 20 years ago. In fact, the insurance company continues to keep it another 15 years to the point in which you would have been 100 years of age. At that time, the interest on your $100,800 has earned the insurance company the tidy sum of $2,809,911. This is $800,000 more than your initial death benefit when you were 25 years old. It is also an amount of money that certainly would have served both you and your children well in all of your retirement years.

Penn State University completed a study in 1993 on term life insurance policies where they discovered that:

- More than 90% of all term policies are terminated or converted. 45% within the first year and 72% within the first 3 years.
- Less than 1 policy in 10 survives the period for which it is written.
- After 15 to 20 years of exposure, less than 1% of all term policies are still in force.
- Only 1% of all term insurance resulted in death claims.

What does this mean? It means that with "term insurance" there is a 99% chance you will pay more than you receive. The following principle comes with all of these factors in mind:

Principle #6:

Term life insurance is not the least expensive way to buy life insurance. In fact, it can be a very costly way to buy life insurance *when all the costs are accounted for*.

Now, don't read this chapter wrong – term life insurance has its place. Term life insurance is necessary to provide the peace of mind that what you plan to happen during your life will happen. It ensures that all of the hopes and dreams you have with and for your family will be achieved even if you are no longer there.

However, there is a better way than spending a lifetime's fortune to achieve this peace of mind.

Chapter 3

Permanent Life Insurance Basics

Permanent life insurance is any life insurance that is guaranteed to pay a death benefit whenever your life ends, provided that you pay the policy premiums. Perhaps the most striking feature of a permanent life insurance policy is that the premium does not increase with age. The premium does not increase with age because, generally, permanent life insurance asks you to commit to a higher premium in your early years of life when the insurance company's cost of providing a death benefit is still low.

Because of these larger premiums paid early on in life, permanent life insurance also includes "cash value." Cash value is what the life insurance contract is worth (less any surrender charges, if applicable) if you decide to terminate the policy before death. Without terminating the policy, cash value provides numerous other living benefits which is discussed at length later in this book. Be aware that if you terminate the contract, what you receive in excess of what your cumulative premiums have been is taxable income. The cash value is calculated by first determining the portion of the premiums you have paid in excess to the *cost* of providing the death benefit (an excess otherwise known as "excess premium"). That amount is then added to the previous year's cash value. Finally, the insurance company adds any interest or dividends (if declared by the insurance company) that the policyholder elected to allow to compound inside the life insurance policy. Put more simply, the cash value is any excess premiums in the policy plus any interest and dividends in the policy.

In the later years of your life, rather than having exponentially increasing policy premiums, it is the annual premiums you continue to pay; in addition to the dividends your policy has been compounding, and any "excess premiums" from your earlier years that will pay the cost of providing the death benefit. Some permanent life insurance policies strive to have as little cash value as possible at death and others strive to use the cash value as a retirement accumulation account that can be accessed tax free to support or supplement your retirement lifestyle. Regardless of the permanent policy, the following principle holds true:

Principle #7:

The more money paid into a permanent policy the better.

To illustrate, I am going to use an example where the premium for a $2,000,000 term life insurance policy for a healthy 35 year old is $385 for each of the first 10 years, and where a new term policy is applied for each 10-year period thereafter. However, we need to make a major change. When you own a permanent life insurance policy, your health never has to be reevaluated. Your annual premium for the rest of your life is determined by your health when you first applied for the policy, in this case age 35. The cost of insurance still goes up each year based your age, but the health that your premium is calculated on never changes. Realistically, a 90-year-old on their deathbed will have the next year's cost of insurance determined by their health when they were 35. For this example we are going to consider the following costs of providing the death benefit:

- Ages 35–44: $385 per year
- Ages 45–54: $1,005 per year
- Ages 55–64: $2,905 per year
- Ages 65–74: $8,645 per year, and so on until death

Though the *cost* of the policy is listed in the schedule above, the *premium* for a $2,000,000 permanent life insurance policy is a steady $18,895 per year. This policy guarantees the $2,000,000 death benefit through age 121.

Again, cash value is the difference between the premium paid ($18,895) and the cost of the insurance (see the schedule above). These "excess premiums" may be granted dividends if declared by the insurance company that you can allow to compound, thereby increasing the cash value. So, at age 65 - using this policy's figures - you will have paid $566,850 of premiums. And let's say that you allowed all dividends granted to continue to be reinvested and compounded during the life of the policy. Even with the insurance company deducting the cost of the insurance (see the schedule above), *the cash value alone at age 65 would be over $1,000,000!* And all along providing your family with $2,000,000 of death benefits to replace your income should you pass away prior to age 65.

There are two questions that the previous example raises:

1. What did it really cost to provide $2,000,000 of death benefits for the past 30 years? Let's see, you paid $566,850 and you could cash in the

policy and receive $1,051,778 (at 2013 dividend rates). Rather than there being an overall financial outlay, there is an overall financial gain of $484,928, less any applicable taxes.

2. What would you do with this extra $1,000,000? There are a number of options that we will explore, but one of them could be to use the $1,000,000 to supplement your retirement lifestyle while maintaining the death benefit so that your beneficiaries would still receive the death benefit at your death.

The above example uses the facts and figures of a 2013 permanent life insurance contract. The 2013 dividend is projected into the future assuming that the same level of dividend would be paid for the life of the contract. Future dividends and costs of insurance could vary.

Still, in this simple example, you can see that in order to own a permanent life insurance policy you must have the ability to add significant funds to the contract each year. However, if you do, some pretty amazing things can happen.

Chapter 4

Types of Permanent Life Insurance Policies

Over the years, permanent life insurance has evolved from the original permanent policy, whole life insurance. Among the features these newer permanent policies have integrated in the original design, is how the cash value dividends are calculated.

Whole Life Insurance

The distinguishing mark of whole life insurance is that, if funded as designed, it is guaranteed to pay a death benefit no matter how long you live. The policy discussed in the last chapter is an example of a whole life insurance policy. Whole life insurance is the oldest form of permanent life insurance. It is tried and true, and remains the most stable of all life insurance available.

Whole life insurance cash values are invested as a general asset of the life insurance company and the policy may be credited with dividends each year if dividends are declared by the insurance company. There may be a contractual guaranteed dividend that must be paid yearly, and any additional dividends granted also become guaranteed once they are added to your account. In other words, after a dividend has been granted it cannot be taken away.

Universal Life Insurance

Traditional universal life insurance was designed at a time in U.S. economic history when interest rates were on the rise. The thought was that if the premiums for universal life insurance were segregated and invested separately from the assets of the insurance company, then something greater than the dividend of a whole life insurance policy could be added to the cash value balance. If greater interest rates could be achieved, then premiums could be lower. In fact, premiums might even be able to fluctuate.

Giving the consumer the ability to vary the level of premiums, sponsoring life insurance companies could not issue the life insurance with the guarantees of whole life insurance. Universal life insurance policies lack the assurance of whole life insurance policy guarantees. However, once a premium is reduced, a policy owner expects it to stay reduced and any increase in the level of the premium is not a welcome thought. To keep universal life insurance in the permanent life insurance category, premiums must be of an adequate level to permanently sustain the promised death benefits.

Variable universal life insurance was designed when interest rates were falling and the stock market was on the rise. Surely, what couldn't be earned via traditional interest might be earned in the stock market. The roaring 1990's proved this theory right, but then came 2000-2002 when the market crashed and then again in 2008.

Other than where the money is invested, variable universal life insurance works the same way as the traditional universal life insurance design. The biggest difference between the two is that while traditional universal life insurance may receive a low level of interest, variable universal life insurance cash values may actually lose money if the investments that the policy owner chooses perform poorly. A dramatic drop in value could lapse the policy in a very short matter of time. A minimally funded contract is easy to lose control of. (For a prospectus regarding a Variable Universal Life contract, contact your investment advisor).

Indexed universal life insurance is a blend of the traditional universal life insurance (based on interest rates) and variable universal life insurance (based on stock market returns including market losses). Indexed universal life insurance usually attempts to track a stock market index while guaranteeing that if the market suffers a decline, the indexed universal life insurance cash value will not lose money. This method uses upside caps, limiting the upside of market gains while utilizing a hedging strategy that eliminates the downside of stock market investments.

Principle #8:

The only difference between the different universal life insurance contracts is in their methods of investment.

Chapter 5

Permanent Life
Insurance Funding Limits

There is a minimum amount of money that you can pay for your life insurance and there is a maximum that you can pay. The life insurance company determines the minimum amount that you can pay. The life insurance company does this by studying the probability that a death benefit will be paid out and then determining the necessary premium to cover this cost and still make the life insurance company a profit. It is the U.S. government that determines the maximum amount of money that you can put into your life insurance contract.

Principle #9:

If the government wants to limit something that I want to do, then it's probably in my best interest to do as much of it as they will allow!

Now stop for a minute and think about why the U.S. government might want to put a limit on something. The reason is probably because "that something" has certain advantages for you that put the government at corresponding disadvantages. In this case, the overarching advantage or disadvantage that concerns the government relates to taxes.

By law, death benefits paid by a life insurance company come to the insured completely *income tax* free. In fact, there is nowhere to even indicate the amount of death benefits received on an income tax return. To be completely clear – I am speaking about income taxes, not estate taxes. Life insurance proceeds must still be reported on the deceased's estate tax returns.

In addition, distributions from a life insurance policy during the life of the insured may also not be reportable for income tax purposes. In other words, you are always entitled to withdraw your premiums tax-free (you received no tax deduction when you made the payments), however, any growth over and above the premiums is taxed when withdrawn. This growth is taxed UNLESS the distributions are taken in the form of a loan against the policy. Outstanding loans against the death benefit at the time of death will be collected from the death benefits.

Just like any loan, a loan against your life insurance policy is not income. Think about when you bought your home and you applied for and received a mortgage. The amount of the mortgage is what the bank loaned you so that you could purchase your home. Was the amount of the mortgage reported as taxable income that year? No. The same was true when you purchased your last vehicle. Did the loan that enabled that purchase wind up on your income tax return? No. The same is true for any loan, whether for college expenses, weddings, vacations, or computer purchases. Loan proceeds are not taxable income and it doesn't matter where the loan comes from (your local bank, the car dealership, your insurance company, etc.).

Principle #10:

If I have a permanent life insurance policy, then I have a new source of potentially income tax free cash when I need it: from the life insurance company that issued my permanent insurance policy.

Now, anything *that* good must be limited by the government. They don't want us to have too much of a good thing. In the 1980's, the government "drew the line" that determined the "maximum" amount of contributions allowable for a given amount of coverage. They accomplished this with two laws: TAMRA and DEFRA (Technical and Miscellaneous Revenue Act of 1988 and Deficit Reduction Act of 1984). These two laws basically said, "slow it down." The government could not continue to let people put unlimited contributions in a life insurance policy because if people did, income tax revenues would decline. Worse yet, the government realized that if they didn't do something about this, they would never receive the tax revenue because of the tax-free nature of death benefits and cash flows from the life insurance companies in the form of loans to the policyholders. TAMRA and DEFRA effectively determine that if money placed into a life insurance policy exceeds the maximum line, the life insurance contract in many ways will be treated as a "qualified plan." The government prefers that you put your money into a "qualified retirement plan account" and *postpone* the taxes rather than avoid the income taxes all together. Samples of qualified retirement plan accounts include: 401(k), IRA, SEP, and 403(b) plans (just to name a few).

Now, there are many reasons in my opinion why "qualified plans" are so important to the government. For one, in the period that you are "deferring taxes," you are probably a better investor for the government than the government is for itself. And, of course, the longer they wait for you to pay your taxes, the better their investment will likely become. But there is another reason that is even more important: as they wait for you to pay your taxes, you are also deferring *the tax calculation*.

What does this mean? Let's say you wanted to borrow $10,000 from the bank. You walk in to the bank and you ask for the money. They explain that you first need to make your request in writing, describing why you want the money and why you will be able to pay back the money. You fill out the application and take the application to the bank. Then they discuss whether you are worthy and whether they have enough money to give you. Now let's suppose the bank has plenty of money in the vault and they offer you the $10,000. You would want to ask two questions before you took their money: "how much interest do I have to pay?" and "when do I have to pay it back?" If the bank responded by saying, "we have enough money right now and do not need any payments from you at this time, but there will come a time when we will need the money, and that is when you will need to pay it back. When we know how much we need, we will be able to determine how much interest we will charge you in order to get the amount we need." Would you cash that check? Absolutely not! But this is exactly what we are doing when we invest our money in "qualified retirement accounts." For every deposit into a 401(k) or IRA, we are borrowing the taxes otherwise due today and agreeing to pay those taxes when the government wants them and at whatever tax rate the government wants to charge at that time. The government is NOT saying: "you do not owe the tax." They are only saying: "you can pay the tax later." What tax bracket will you be in "later?" That is a good question. This is not to say qualified plans are all bad. However, it is important that you know and understand exactly what they do, and why there is a limit to how much money you can put into your life insurance policy.

Principle #11:

There is so much more that a permanent life insurance contract can do for me than just provide a death benefit.

In 1997, during the Clinton Presidential Administration, the Taxpayer Relief Act was passed by over 90% of Congress and signed into law by President Clinton. "The TRA of '97," as it would become known, provided many new tax benefits encouraging: home ownership, college education, larger families, and retirement savings. It is this law that brought about the ROTH IRA. Now, instead of taking a tax deduction and postponing paying the taxes to a future date at whatever the tax rate is then, the ROTH IRA took away the current tax deduction in exchange for excusing all of the taxes that otherwise would be due on the growth.

Leading up to the passage of TRA '97, the discussion in Washington D.C. might have gone something like this: "let's design a plan that will encourage Americans to save in a retirement fund that they will be able to use without incurring a tax. If we were to design the perfect plan, what would that look like?" Then they listed the following 13 characteristics of this plan:

1. The plan should allow for a tax deduction for all money saved in the plan.
2. The plan should allow for tax-deferred growth.
3. The plan should provide for income tax-free withdrawals.
4. The plan should make competitive returns possible.
5. The plan should allow any taxpayer to put in as much money as they want.
6. The plan should provide a taxpayer to use the account as collateral for a loan.
7. The plan should protect against market losses.
8. The plan should assure access to loans should the taxpayer need money before age 59 ½.
9. The plan should allow for these loans to be paid at the taxpayer's discretion.
10. The plan should be protected from creditors.
11. The plan should eliminate early withdrawal penalties, late withdrawal penalties, and excess contribution penalties – there just shouldn't be any penalties at all.
12. The government should continue the contributions to the plan at the same level the taxpayer was contributing if the taxpayer should become disabled and can't continue to put money into the plan.
13. The government should accelerate the expected retirement account balance to the taxpayer's family if the taxpayer dies prior to retirement.

The Senators and Representatives may have huddled together and said "with all these benefits, who wouldn't save for retirement? But we can't give away the 'farm.'" So they removed the proposal for the contributions to the plan each year to be tax deductible, leaving the last 12 listed above. They studied the proposal, submitted it to the Government Accounting Office for their analysis of future economic effects, and were ready to go until one of the congressmen said: "wait – this looks just like permanent life insurance." Upon that revelation Congress stripped out items 5-13 and called it a ROTH IRA.

This story is obviously not the way it occurred, but it does humorously demonstrate the difference between permanent life insurance and a ROTH IRA. It also demonstrates the benefits you ought to demand from a life insurance company if they are going to expect you to put $10,000 a year into a policy instead of $100 per year for term insurance.

Chapter 6

Life Insurance Policy Riders

A life insurance contract can include more than just a death benefit. When you purchase a life insurance policy, further benefits can be optionally added to a basic policy in the form of a "rider." A rider is an attachment to the basic death benefit that gives options to assure that a death benefit is always available and affordable. Insurance policy riders are available with both term and permanent life insurance. Some of these riders can give you additional benefits and increase peace of mind that - if something goes wrong - there's a "plan b." Other riders enhance the financial strategies that life insurance can bring to your other retirement assets. Riders vary by insurance company and policy, as do the rules for how they work. Costs also vary and depend on many factors including your age, health, and type of policy. This chapter gives a brief overview a few of the riders you ought to consider when purchasing a life insurance contract.

A *guaranteed insurability rider* will allow you to purchase additional coverage even if your health has declined. Perhaps your income has gone up and you want more life insurance. Perhaps you've added a family member through birth or adoption. Perhaps you are on your deathbed and you just want more. This rider lets you purchase additional life insurance coverage at specific dates or events without undergoing a medical exam or providing any evidence about your insurability. When the option comes up to buy more coverage, the insurance company considers your age for setting the premium, but not your health.

An *accelerated death benefit rider* is beneficial in the event that you become terminally ill. This rider is usually included automatically for free or offered at a nominal cost. The rider lets you collect a portion of the policy's death benefit if you become terminally ill with a short life expectancy (such as one year). The policy spells out how much of the death benefit is available before death. Usually it's capped at $250,000 to $500,000. You can use these proceeds for anything: paying medical bills, living expenses, experimental health treatments not covered by your health insurance plan, or even an around the world cruise with your loved one. Even though the insurer may offer the rider for free, the company may also charge a fee if it is exercised. But as we have learned before, it is better to have and not need than to need and not have - especially if there is no charge to have it available.

A *critical illness rider* will prove beneficial if you should become critically ill. Perhaps it is not a terminal illness that you develop, but one of those illnesses that linger on with great expense. Similar to the accelerated death benefit rider, the insurer will pay an agreed amount of the death benefits early to finance some of those long-term care expenses.

A *child or family protection rider*: in case the unthinkable happens. No one wants to consider the possibility of losing a child, so all emotion must be set aside when considering a child protection rider. Although the death of a child typically would not result in income loss like the death of a spouse, the tragedy still would have some financial consequences that could be an additional hardship for a bereaved family. This rider provides temporary term insurance coverage for final expenses. The coverage generally can be purchased in units – for example, $1,000 at a nominal price. Basic information about the child's health is required for underwriting.

An *accidental death benefit rider* is a benefit in case you die from an accident. In the event of accidental death, this rider provides an additional benefit on top of the policy's regular death benefit. Sometimes the rider also includes additional payment for dismemberment. You would collect money if you lost a limb or your sight. However, if you choose a rider like this make sure you ask yourself the question, "is my economic human life value different if I die in an automobile accident or if I die of a heart attack"? An accidental death benefit rider should not be purchased *in lieu of* insurance that will pay a death benefit regardless of the style of death.

The final two policy riders discussed in this chapter add both great economic and great emotional value to your life insurance policy.

A *convertibility rider* is a provision that allows you to convert your term policy to a permanent life insurance policy without having your health rescreened for pricing and issuance purposes. This conversion can be done within a specified period of time for an amount equal to the amount of the term policy.

In order to understand the importance of the "convertibility" rider, let's look at an example of a 35-year-old man, Barry, who DID NOT purchase a term life insurance policy with this feature. We will assume that Barry's economic human life value is $2,000,000, and we will examine two possible scenarios of Barry's future:

Scenario 1: Barry's plan is to spend as little as possible on a life insurance policy. Barry purchases a term life insurance policy with premiums that stay level and low for the first ten years and then increase in cost each year thereafter. Once the first ten years have passed and Barry is at the end of the level premium portion of his term policy, the $385 cost per year is about to go up to $9,405 in year 11 and more every year thereafter. During the last ten years Barry has also started to smoke. Barry's alternative now is to take a new term policy, but no longer at the best insurance rates once the insurance company realizes that he has picked up the habit of smoking. Now, the new 10-year term policy is no longer $385 a year, but now $8,565. This is still cheaper than $9,405 a year for Barry to keep his current term policy, but it's still a fairly discouraging number. Additionally, after another 10 years he has the same decision to make, but to continue this new term policy it will now cost $19,945!

However, if Barry had originally purchased the convertibility rider, the $385 per year cost would have given him more options and cost only $20 extra each year. The convertibility rider would allow Barry to convert the term policy to a permanent policy that would require level premium payments of $8,952 for the rest of his life. In many permanent policies, insurance companies pay interest or dividends on accumulated cash balances inside the life insurance contract. If Barry did convert to a permanent policy, at current dividend rates (dividend rates range from 5% -7%, I am assuming 6%) he would receive a death benefit of $2,000,000 as long as he continued paying $8,952 per year up to age 87.

Scenario 2: Barry's life has gone according to plan, meaning he is still in the best of health at age 55 when he purchases his last term life insurance policy. However, toward the conclusion of this last term policy at age 64, Barry is diagnosed with terminal cancer and he isn't expected to live more than another 5 years. Barry can keep his original plan in place and surrender the term policy, but after coming to terms with his shortened life expectancy, Barry realizes that keeping his term policy is now a significant investment opportunity for his family. If Barry keeps this last term policy, having paid $2,905 for each of the last 10 years, the cost to continue the policy in year 11 is $61,965. This seems like a lot, but for a redemption value of $2,000,000 (a 3,000% rate of return) it is a good investment. If Barry lives past the eleventh year, the twelfth year premium is $68,125, which is still a two-year rate of return of 1,400%. If Barry lives twice the number of years his doctor first estimated (10 more years), his rate of return is still more than 10% per year on average. The return might be great, but the problem it presents is complex:

- First, each year Barry is faced with having to reconsider his diagnosis and his mortality even though he is "beating it."
- Second, Barry will need to pump over $970,000 into the term life insurance policy and he might live longer than another 10 years. Of course if he dies, his beneficiary will receive $2,000,000.
- Third, if Barry stops funding the life insurance policy at any point after paying that eleventh year premium, he will make the previous year's decision to pay the premium a poor financial decision.
- Fourth, as Barry pays the premiums each year and lives off of his nest egg, what is the status of his nest egg?

If the original term policy had the "term to permanent" insurance conversion rider, the smoking decision and the cancer diagnosis would not have been an issue. The rider would have provided alternatives to Barry that would not have been available if the rider had not been purchased in the original first term insurance policy.

For Barry, the economic value in the convertibility rider comes from being able to keep the level of death benefit for a set future cost that will never change despite health changes. There is also emotional value in the rider for Barry, as he will not be forced to revisit his mortality each year should he ever have to "beat" a disease. The consideration each year of paying another enormous premium alone could be hazardous to Barry's health.

Principle #12:

There is both *economic* and *emotional* value in the "convertibility rider" of a term life insurance policy.

A *waiver of premium rider* is another rider that brings both sizeable economic and emotional value to your life insurance policy. This is a rider that can help you should you ever become disabled. Studies by the Social Security Administration demonstrate that a 20-year-old worker has a 30% chance of becoming disabled before he or she reaches retirement age (www.ltdrates.com). A 40-year-old male is twice as likely to become disabled before the age of 65 than he is to die before the age of 65 (http://www.protectyourincome.com/education-center/disability-facts-and-statistics/probability). Given the previous example regarding the convertibility rider (with the same person who was unexpectedly diagnosed with cancer), the disability waiver would eliminate the continual "investment" of future premiums until the eventual $2,000,000 payoff at death. Now that is a rate of return we can't even calculate!

So, the economic value of the "disability waiver of premium rider" comes from not having to make continual premium payments during years of lower income levels because of disability. But, the rider also carries emotional value by giving the peace of mind that when the eventual death occurs, the hopes of future dreams will still live on without the additional monetary outlays.

Principle #13:

There is *also* both sizeable economic and emotional value in the disability waiver of premium rider of a life insurance policy.

These last two riders make the payment of an eventual death benefit much more likely than it would be without them. As we will learn in the rest of the book, the existence of a permanent death benefit also brings greater value to your other retirement assets as you design your retirement cash flow possibilities.

PART II

How Life Insurance Works

Chapter 7

The Miracle of Compound Interest

There is one basic concept about how money works that is vastly ignored – uninterrupted compound interest! Notice the word "uninterrupted." This is the part that everyone misses. Those of us in the finance industry have been taught our entire lives that the "8th Wonder of the World is compound interest." The original *Confessions of a CPA* book exposes the weakness of compound interest: namely, interrupting the compounding. If you have not read this first book, I urge you to read it now.

Life Insurance is one product that is easy to leave alone, allowing the interest to compound without interruption. How is that so? I have told you that you can access funds represented by the cash values of your life insurance, but won't that interrupt the compounding? The answer is no, you can't interrupt the compounding unless you actually surrender all or a portion of your life insurance; taking a distribution FROM your cash values. The next chapters of this book will help you understand what it means to borrow AGAINST your cash values and not FROM them. This is the key to maintaining uninterrupted compound interest in your account.

But for now, there is another frequently misunderstood basic concept that we need to discover the truth about if we are to understand how life insurance works. That concept is debt. We are often told that debt is bad, and in many cases that is true since debt occurs when we buy things we cannot afford. But in reality, we purchase everything we buy with borrowed money. We either pay someone else interest, or we give up the ability to earn interest. And to top that off, every dollar spent and not saved will never earn uninterrupted compound interest again. It is gone - it is in someone else's coffer earning them interest instead. Every time we spend a dollar, we transfer the potential miracle of compound interest to someone else.

Oh, young love … for many it is inevitable that boy meets girl, boy falls in love with girl, and boy buys a $5,000 diamond ring. Assuming this is a "wise" boy, he has saved up for this day. Let's think about what that ring really costs. If he purchased this ring after his first year out of college, at age 23, what would his $5,000 have been worth years down the road? Assuming that interest rates are never higher than they have been in 2013 (at an all-time low saving interest rates of 1%), then that ring cost the "wise" boy $7,593 of his potential retirement at age 65. Now that is not a big difference and it may be a cost he is willing to pay for 42 years of married bliss, but interest rates haven't and won't remain at 1%. In 2008 the savings rate was 3.33% (www.bankrate.com). At that rate over the 42 years of marriage the ring actually cost $19,791. Hmm… Since 1979 the long-term taxable money market rate has averaged 5.7% (www.census.gov/compendia/statab/2012/tables). *Assuming that this is what this boy is giving up in exchange for this lovely ring, the true cost of the ring is $51,300 out of his potential retirement nest egg. By his life expectancy of age 85, that ring has cost his beneficiaries $155,460! Every dollar not saved is consumed by lifestyle, and the compound interest potential of each spent dollar is transferred to someone else.* By the way, if you ever want grandchildren, don't show this book to your son until after he makes his purchase.

This is just an example of buying a diamond ring, but how many other financial choices do we make each day that have the same effect? We transfer wealth every day through necessary and responsible things such as auto insurance, health insurance, college educations, cars, taxes, term life insurance, and the list goes on.

We default into being debtors, where we borrow to spend then work to pay back. When we are trained to be savers, we work to save and we save to spend. Either way we end up at zero. Your goal ought to be wealth creation where you work to save and use other people's money to spend, leaving your savings alone to compound uninterrupted into the future. In order to do this you must have an asset that a financial institution values to collateralize your loan.

Let's spend a bit more time on the true cost of paying cash, which is something we do because we have been taught that this is better than going into debt. If you were to save $5,000 per year at a 5% earning rate, in 30 years you would have $353,804. However, in 4 years you begin to notice that your account balance has grown to more than what you put in the account. In fact, it has $21,550.62 in it. That is $20,000 of your savings plus interest of $1,500 and $50.62 of "miracle" (compounding). But you are driving down the road past an automobile dealership and you discover that you could trade your car plus your $20,000 saved plus your $1,500 of interest earned plus your $50.62 of miracle-to-date for a new car. By emptying your savings tank now for this car, you will now only have $273,346 after 30 years of interest. This means that the real opportunity cost of that car is $80,458 over a 30-year period. But, we don't buy a car just once - we do it over and over again. If you trade your car in and add your savings to the purchase every 4 years, what will you have in 30 years? You will have a four-year-old car and no money in the account. Your cars over 30 years would have cost you your entire $353,804. Remember, that is $150,000 of your savings, plus $153,804 of earned interest and compounding. It doesn't matter whether you save to spend or you borrow to spend, you end up with the same result, $0!

When you use debt, you are borrowing from your future earnings; and when you pay cash you are borrowing from your past savings. If you borrow from your savings, you ought to be saying, "but I can pay myself back." True, and some people do, but they only put back the principle. In our car example they put back $20,000, which is the amount that they had saved, but they forget about the interest. Few people pay back their principle *and* interest. If you are one of these people, then good for you. But no one pays back the principle, the interest, *and* the compounding. No one does this because it is a very difficult calculation to make - if you are making payments to yourself over time, the compounding continues to be lost over the payback period. However, this is the only way to truly reset the miracle.

———————

Principle #14:

A penny saved is more than a penny earned because the earnings compound exponentially (but only if I leave the compounding alone).

———————

What if you could make a purchase without disturbing your compounding account? You would not lose the benefits of compounding.

But if you don't use your money, whose money do you use? I'm glad you asked.

Chapter 8

Using Other People's Money

If you don't use your money, whose do you use? I bet you think I'm going to say your life insurance cash values. Nope. But you are close. This is a basic financial principle not only available from your life insurance company. The life insurance company that has underwritten your life insurance policy is one option, but there are others. This money is available from any financial institution that will allow you to borrow their money by securing the loan by pledging a portion of your compounding interest account. It may be a money market account at that same bank. It could be your house, your mutual fund, or 401(k) plan.

Here is how it works:

You set up an account that you pour money into on a regular basis. When it is time to make a large purchase - a diamond ring, a car, a college education - you contact your favorite financial institution. They will have a form for you to fill out; it is only a couple of pages long asking you things like your income, your total assets, what other loans you have outstanding, if there is a cosigner on the account, and if you have any collateral to pledge. Basically, this is information to tell the financial institution that you really don't need the money. If your application is deficient in any way, your loan request will be denied. There is a section at the end labeled

"For Lender's Use Only." Here you learn that your application needs to be approved by an officer of the institution or a loan committee. It is interesting that there are five decisions they can make regarding your request, and only one is in your favor. Besides approving your loan, they can deny it by determining that they need more information, make a counter offer, or give you conditional approval.

Assuming they approve your loan application, they will set up a loan repayment schedule to their liking – a schedule that will pay back your loan with interest in a given amount of time. Deviate from this schedule (other than accelerating it), and they will collect the collateral from you. In other words, they will come get the diamond ring, or they will activate the GPS that was attached to your car so they can find it. You think I'm kidding – I'm not! Think of it as an ankle bracelet for your car. But assuming all goes well, at the end of the repayment schedule you will still have your car and your compounding interest account will have remained untouched with the entire miracle (compounding) still in it.

If you are saying, "but I've paid interest to use the bank's money," go back and reread the compounding interest chapter until you understand that every purchase you make is financed, even if you pay cash. You either pay interest or you don't earn interest. Either way, it is the same.

Chapter 9

Accounts You Can Collateralize

Let's go back to the chapter "Permanent Life Insurance Basics" when I poked a little bit of fictional fun on the debate around the development of a ROTH IRA. When trying to design the perfect account, you would want the following ideal characteristics:

1. The account should allow for tax deductions for all the money saved in the account.
2. The account should allow for tax-deferred growth.
3. The account should provide for income tax-free distributions.
4. The account should make competitive returns possible.
5. The account should allow any taxpayer to put in as much money as they want.
6. The account should provide a taxpayer to use the account as collateral for a loan.
7. The account should protect against losses.
8. The account should assure access to loans should the taxpayer need money before age 59 ½.
9. The account should allow for these loans to be paid at the taxpayer's discretion.
10. The account should be protected from creditors.

11. The account should eliminate early withdrawal penalties, late withdrawal penalties, and excess contribution penalties – there just shouldn't be any penalties at all.

12. The government should continue the contributions to the plan at the same level that the taxpayer was contributing if the taxpayer should become disabled and can't continue to put money into the plan.

13. The government should accelerate the expected retirement account balance to the taxpayer's family if the taxpayer dies unexpectedly prior to retirement.

Principle #15:

If you are going to collateralize an account to secure a *structured loan*, you want to collateralize the account with the least number of ideal account attributes.

If these were the characteristics of an ideal account, an account with something less than these characteristics would be the account that you would want to collateralize if the financial institution would accept it. If you are going to trade the use and control of an account for a loan that is subject to structured payments and rules, you want to tie up your least valuable account.

While there are many accounts that will work, not all are created equal. Listed with each of the potential accounts are the 13 ideal characteristics, the characteristics that don't pertain to the product have been "lined out" so you can see how far from ideal they are. Let's look at a few of these accounts:

Traditional Banking Products: Savings, Money Market Accounts, and Certificates of Deposit

1. ~~The account should allow for tax deductions for all the money saved in the account.~~
2. ~~The account should allow for tax-deferred growth.~~
3. The account should provide for income tax-free distributions.
4. ~~The account should make competitive returns possible.~~
5. The account should allow any taxpayer to put in as much money as they want.
6. The account should allow a taxpayer to use the account as collateral for a loan.
7. The account should protect against losses.
8. ~~The account should assure access to loans should the taxpayer need money before age 59 ½.~~
9. ~~The account should allow for these loans to be paid by at the taxpayer's discretion.~~
10. ~~The account should be protected from creditors.~~
11. ~~The account should eliminate early withdrawal penalties, late withdrawal penalties, and excess contribution penalties – there just shouldn't be any penalties at all.~~ Certificates of Deposit are the only accounts in this category that have early withdrawal penalties.
12. ~~The government should continue the contributions to the plan at the same level the taxpayer was contributing, if the taxpayer should~~

~~become disabled and can't continue to put money into the plan.~~

~~13. The government should accelerate the expected retirement account balance to the taxpayer's family if the taxpayer dies unexpectedly prior to retirement.~~

Traditional banking products display four out of the 13 ideal account characteristics – not bad, but not great. This means that savings accounts, money market accounts, and certificates of deposit would be great candidates for putting up as collateral to secure a structured loan.

Traditional Retirement Plans such as a 401(k)

This is an account that can be directly borrowed from. Your loan will be from the qualified retirement plan itself. 401(k) loan provisions are governed by the IRS.

1. The account should allow for tax deductions for all the money saved in the account.
2. The account should allow for tax-deferred growth.
3. ~~The account should provide for income tax-free distributions.~~
4. The account should make competitive returns possible.
5. ~~The account should allow any taxpayer to put in as much money as they want.~~
6. ~~The account should allow a taxpayer to use the account as collateral for a loan.~~
7. ~~The account should protect against losses.~~
8. ~~The account should assure access to loans should the taxpayer need money before age 59 ½~~ *(not all 401(k) plans are approved for loans).*

9. ~~The account should allow for these loans to be paid by at the taxpayer's discretion.~~
10. The account should be protected from creditors.
11. ~~The account should eliminate early withdrawal penalties, late withdrawal penalties, and excess contribution penalties — there just shouldn't be any penalties at all.~~
12. ~~The government should continue the contributions to the plan at the same level the taxpayer was contributing, if the taxpayer should become disabled and can't continue to put money into the plan.~~
13. ~~The government should accelerate the expected retirement account balance to the taxpayer's family if the taxpayer dies unexpectedly prior to retirement.~~

Traditional retirement plans display four out of the 13 ideal account characteristics. A 401(k) or any qualified plan account is the only type of account where the money put into the plan is tax-deferred. However, beware: the distributions from a qualified plan are immediately taxable when taken out. Since the tax rate may be higher when the money is *taken* from the account than when the money was *put into* the account, this makes the advantage of tax deductibility questionable. It may depend on how much your account has grown because account earnings are tax-deferred as well.

With only three of the 13 characteristics (one of which is questionable), this makes a traditional retirement plan account a likely asset to collateralize toward a structured loan.

However, the loan terms are determined by the IRS, and are more restrictive in too main ways. First, the length of the repayment is fixed depending on whether the loan is for the purchase of a house or for some other purpose. Second, if you leave your employment and don't repay the loan in full at the time of your termination, the government will deem that the loan was not a loan, but a distribution subject to all of the taxes and penalties for early withdrawal. This second restriction is possibly the most disastrous loan provision ever designed (and accepted by millions of Americans, 20% of 401(k) participants have outstanding loans http://www.forbes.com/sites/ashleaebeling/2013/07/12/coming-employer-crackdown-on-401k-loans/).

Real Estate Equity via a Home Equity Line of Credit

This is a loan based on the equity you have in your home. The value of your home itself is the collateral for the loan.

1. ~~The account should allow for tax deductions for all the money saved in the account.~~
2. The account should allow for tax-deferred growth.
3. ~~The account should provide for income tax-free distributions.~~
4. ~~The account should make competitive returns possible.~~
5. ~~The account should allow any taxpayer to put in as much money as they want.~~
6. The account should allow a taxpayer to use the account as collateral for a loan.
7. ~~The account should protect against losses.~~
8. ~~The account should assure access to loans should the taxpayer need money before age 59 ½.~~
9. ~~The account should allow for these loans to be paid by at the taxpayer's discretion.~~
10. ~~The account should be protected from creditors.~~
11. ~~The account should eliminate early withdrawal penalties, late withdrawal penalties, and excess~~

~~contribution penalties – there just shouldn't be any penalties at all.~~

~~12. The government should continue the contributions to the plan at the same level the taxpayer was contributing, if the taxpayer should become disabled and can't continue to put money into the plan.~~

~~13. The government should accelerate the expected retirement account balance to the taxpayer's family if the taxpayer dies unexpectedly prior to retirement.~~

Real estate equity via a home equity line of credit holds two out of the 13 ideal account characteristics. This would be a good candidate to secure a structured loan if you can get a bank to agree. However, if you have any other debts that the house collateralizes, the home equity line of credit lender would be subordinated to the other lenders. In the housing market decline of 2008-2012, many subordinated lenders were left holding the bag when home equity declined and the collateral itself disappeared into thin air.

Permanent Life Insurance

This is a loan based on the cash values you have in your policy. A financial institution will require that you assign your policy in the case of default of your structured loan.

~~1. The account should allow for tax deductions for all the money saved in the account.~~

2. The account should allow for tax-deferred growth.

3. The account should provide for tax-free distributions.

4. The account should make competitive returns possible.

5. The account should allow any taxpayer to put in as much money as they want.

6. The account should provide a taxpayer to use the account as collateral for a loan.

7. The account should protect against losses. Variable Universal Life contracts do not protect against losses.

8. The account should assure access to loans should the taxpayer need money before age 59 ½.

9. The account should allow for these loans to be paid by at the taxpayer's discretion.

10. The account should be protected from creditors.

11. The account should eliminate early withdrawal penalties, late withdrawal penalties, and excess contribution penalties – there just shouldn't be any penalties at all. Universal Life Insurance contracts may have surrender penalties.

12. The ~~government~~ insurance company should continue the contributions to the plan at the same level the taxpayer was contributing, if the taxpayer should become disabled and can't continue to put money into the plan.

13. The ~~government~~ insurance company should accelerate the death benefit which will exceed the retirement projected cash value. ~~expected retirement account~~ ~~balance~~ to the taxpayer's family if the taxpayer dies unexpectedly prior to retirement.

Wow, depending on the type of permanent life insurance you purchase there may be 12 of the 13 ideal account characteristics!

WARNING: Trick Question Ahead:

True or false: this would also be an ideal account to use as collateral for a secured loan.

FALSE: you don't want to tie up the asset you own with the most potential in terms of value and benefits as collateral for a structured loan.

Now you are probably completely confused. This book is about life insurance and you've led me all the way to this point and the answer is not life insurance?

No, not for a *structured loan*. Life insurance works best when used to collateralize an *unstructured* loan. Why would you want to have to abide by all the restrictions of a conventional loan when you don't have to?

Where do you get an unstructured loan? From the life insurance company that issued your life insurance contract.

The advantage of borrowing against your life insurance policy from your life insurance company is that your permanent life insurance policy has a provision in its contract that obligates the life insurance company to give you an *unstructured* loan. This is a loan without all of the requirements that a structured loan from a conventional lender will require. No lengthy loan application. No approval process, therefore no loan denials. No required repayment of the principle of the loan. No required time period in which to pay back the loan, if ever. The only rights the insurance company has in regard to a loan against your life insurance policy is that they can collect the outstanding loan at your death from the death benefit payable and charge you interest while the loan is outstanding. Even there, you have the right to borrow the interest from the life insurance company as well using your life insurance cash values as collateral.

Should your loan outstanding plus unpaid interest ever exceed your cash value, the life insurance company will cancel both the loan and the policy itself. Cancellation of your policy, will result in the loss of your death benefits and may result in taxable income to the extent that the cash value in the account exceeds your premiums. So, be careful and monitor your loan activity.

Chapter 10

Using Your Life Insurance to Collateralize a Loan

One important point to understand is the difference between a structured loan and an unstructured loan. It is primarily structured loans that were addressed in the previous chapter. This chapter will primarily focus on unstructured loans. Obtaining an unstructured loan is something to which you may not have access. However if you can obtain a unstructured loan, it is likely that you own a permanent life insurance policy or else you are among the very few who can negotiate such a loan with your local bank (although if you are one of these lucky few, you are still leaving wealth potential on the table by not having the permanent life insurance contract, as explained in chapters 11 and 12).

Principle #16:

An unstructured loan has more advantages than a structured loan.

What is an unstructured loan? It is basically an open-ended loan arrangement you have with either a financial institution (few people can obtain this), access to loans from friends without terms, or available from your life insurance company if you own a permanent life insurance contract. It is open-ended because the time and frequency of repayment is not defined. The only thing to negotiate is the interest rate. There are minimal forms to fill out, and you can have your money within a week to 10 days, which is basically the time it takes to cut the check and send it to you.

An unstructured loan is advantageous when there is no set time of repayment. This means that you can pay it back whenever you want! Interest will accrue against the loan, and if you have enough collateral capacity to absorb the loan, you may never have to repay the loan or the interest.

An unstructured loan is also advantageous when the frequency of repayment is flexible. That means you can make monthly payments, skip a payment, double up a payment, suspend payments, or do just about anything you want, as long as you have enough collateral capacity to absorb the financing costs of skipping a payment. The key is: you are in charge. Miss three months payments and your car will not get repossessed. In fact, there is no need for a GPS tracking device!

Principle #17:

Collateral capacity defines how much of an unstructured loan a financial institution will extend to you.

I've mentioned a term you may not be familiar with – collateral capacity. Let me define that for you. It simply means the amount you have in your accounts that can be collateralized. There are three things that can increase your capacity. The first is your deposits into your account. The second is internal growth on funds already in your account. And the third is lien reduction – every payment toward outstanding loans releases collateral capacity dollar for dollar. Now, once you've made all the contributions that the account will hold, once it's growing at its maximum potential, and once you have no liens, your next alternative is to get a larger account.

Notice you are still earning compound interest on money you have in your account including the money you have in a collateral position.

The most powerful asset you can collateralize to access other people's money for an UNSTRUCTURED loan is a permanent life insurance contract. When designed and utilized properly, permanent life insurance can provide stable growth, cash value collateralization, guaranteed loan access, no annual income tax on the growth or the death benefits, as well as other benefits with additional policy riders.

Let's review some of the things you should remember about a permanent life insurance policy:

- Once dividends are paid by your life insurance contract, they become guaranteed cash value if reinvested in the contract. However, there is no guarantee that the life insurance company will declare a dividend.
- Cash value grows tax-deferred.
- Loans are a contract feature. There is no "approval" process and you do not need to

disclose what you plan to use the loan for. The contract is unilateral and provisions can only be changed by the owner. Loans reduce access to available cash value by the amount of the loan.

- Death benefits are paid income tax-free and are reduced by outstanding loans or withdrawals.
- Loan repayments are made at the discretion of the policy owner. The frequency and the amount of the payments is solely at the discretion of the policy owner.
- If done properly, funds can be taken from the policy income tax-free.
- In most states, cash values are protected from creditors.
- Insufficient payments to cover the base premiums may lead to policy lapse and tax consequences.
- Premiums and death benefits are guaranteed.
- A waiver of premium in the case of total disability is available as an optional rider at the time you purchase your life insurance policy at an additional cost. A disability waiver can pay premiums if the insured is unable to work due to sickness or disability when you can't.
- The acceleration of an expected retirement account balance is what a death benefit payable at your death effectively does.
- You are not borrowing your cash value; you are borrowing against your cash values. You are obtaining the life insurance companies money – not yours. This is vitally important. if you were borrowing your money, you would not receive dividends on the amount you had borrowed!

Remember, the key is to leave your money alone so it can compound uninterrupted into the future.

- Some permanent life insurance policies contain surrender penalties if you surrender your policy (different from borrowing from your policy) and unpaid loans and interest on those loans could result in a policy lapse (an involuntary surrender) resulting in taxable income if your cash values exceed the premiums paid.
- Loans against your death benefits are limited to most of your cash surrender value.

The process of obtaining a loan from your life insurance company against your policy values is pretty simple. If the request can't be made by phone, there is a one-page form to fill out – this basically tells them where you want the check sent. You don't have to disclose your income, your assets, or your liabilities. You don't have to tell them what you want the money for. They don't really care if you can pay it back.

The insurance company gives you the loan and only charges interest (the principle payback is up to you). If you have enough collateral capacity, you can let the interest increase the loan and not even pay the interest. The policy allows for a non-structured payback arrangement. You maintain complete use and control of your money.

This flexibility is tried and true. Many people use it every day. I personally learned about this flexibility when I was taught how to replace a vehicle that suddenly needed to be replaced. I had money saved, but didn't want to relinquish that account that represented a lot of hard work to accumulate. I certainly didn't want to enter another debt with the car dealership. I had just paid off the second car and was using that available cash flow to fund a new permanent life insurance contract. Not knowing where to turn, I asked my financial advisor what he thought I ought to do. He suggested a loan against the death benefit of my first permanent life insurance policy. The rest is history.

I'm often asked, "why isn't everyone doing this?" All I can say is that "everyone who understands does".

Principle #18:

Only a permanent life insurance policy provides you with this kind of flexibility.

Chapter 11

The Secret of Wealth Accumulation

One of the most common questions I hear is: "should I pay back the loan?" The simple answer is "yes." If you are in your earnings years, you should pay back your life insurance loans. The answer is "you don't have to" if you are in your retirement years (but make sure you know where your borrowing limit is). You always want your life insurance policy to outlast you. If you lapse your life insurance policy by borrowing too much and not paying enough back, all the dividend growth is taxable in the year you lapse the policy. Ouch!

Principle #19:

Whenever you eliminate a regular expenditure, continue making those payments to yourself.

The secret of wealth accumulation is this – whenever you eliminate a regular expenditure - whether it is some ongoing expense or a debt repayment stream of cash that has satisfied the debt - continue making those payments to yourself. The car payments fit in your budget for 36 months, so keep it in your budget once the 36 months are completed, but pay it to yourself. If you don't, you will find other ways to spend it in ways you don't even realize.

Let's look at a couple of examples of paying back versus not paying back a life insurance loan.

In our first example, let's look at someone who decides that they are going to fund a permanent life insurance contract with the same amount of money that they pay on their mortgage: $1,500 per month. The assumptions in the following illustrations and examples are:

- A 35-year-old person in good health.
- A life insurance policy currently paying a 6% dividend (current dividend rates range from 5% - 7%).
- The 6% dividend is paid every year (future dividend rates are not guaranteed).
- The premium is the actual current premium for a Whole Life Insurance contract. However, it is also hypothetical because Whole Life Insurance contracts can vary in how their benefits are calculated, consequently their premiums can be different. Premiums are also different based on the age and the health of the insured when the contract is started. Whole Life Insurance premiums are guaranteed to never increase after the initial premium is established.

Please refer to the Important Disclosures at the beginning of the book.

Principle #20:

It costs money to live inside.

The following illustration shows how the cash value compounds:

YR	TOTAL ANNUALIZED PREMIUM	CUMULATIVE NET ANNUALIZED OUTLAY	CASH VALUE INCREASE	TOTAL CASH SURRENDER VALUE	TOTAL DEATH BENEFIT
1	18,000.00	18,000.00	13	13	1,334,407
2	18,000.00	36,000.00	401	414	1,336,234
3	18,000.00	54,000.00	8,311	8,726	1,340,098
4	18,000.00	72,000.00	14,183	22,908	1,345,625
5	18,000.00	90,000.00	15,184	38,092	1,352,633
6	18,000.00	108,000.00	16,240	54,333	1,361,063
7	18,000.00	126,000.00	17,299	71,631	1,370,808
8	18,000.00	144,000.00	18,399	90,031	1,381,868
9	18,000.00	162,000.00	19,519	109,550	1,394,150
10	18,000.00	180,000.00	22,018	131,567	1,412,274
11	18,000.00	198,000.00	24,789	156,356	1,435,694
12	18,000.00	216,000.00	27,410	183,766	1,464,004
13	18,000.00	234,000.00	30,066	213,832	1,496,686
14	18,000.00	252,000.00	32,919	246,751	1,533,352
15	18,000.00	270,000.00	35,855	282,605	1,573,598
16	18,000.00	288,000.00	38,749	321,354	1,617,026
17	18,000.00	306,000.00	41,718	363,072	1,663,377
18	18,000.00	324,000.00	44,609	407,681	1,712,279
19	18,000.00	342,000.00	47,593	455,274	1,763,535
20	18,000.00	360,000.00	50,539	505,813	1,816,901
21	18,000.00	378,000.00	54,222	560,035	1,874,154
22	18,000.00	396,000.00	57,299	617,334	1,933,249
23	18,000.00	414,000.00	60,411	677,745	1,994,000
24	18,000.00	432,000.00	63,816	741,561	2,056,263
25	18,000.00	450,000.00	67,236	808,797	2,119,901
26	18,000.00	468,000.00	65,510	874,307	2,184,862
27	18,000.00	486,000.00	68,381	942,688	2,251,112
28	18,000.00	504,000.00	71,097	1,013,785	2,318,644
29	18,000.00	522,000.00	73,743	1,087,528	2,387,323
30	18,000.00	540,000.00	76,511	1,164,039	2,457,277

This illustration is based on the same policy assumptions discussed earlier.
Hypothetical illustrations should not be used to predict or project investment results.

The first thing to notice is that it costs money to live inside! This is not an "either/or" choice. You don't either own a home with a mortgage or buy a life insurance contract. Given the choice, I will live inside every time. However, seeing how the deposits and interest compound over time, I may want to look for other money that I am either unknowingly or unnecessarily transferring away.

Look at the cash value projection at year 30 - the year you will have also paid off your mortgage – it's over $1.1 million! As long as you purchased the life insurance policy at the same time as you purchased your home, that $1.1 million is yours. The other $1,500 per month that represents your mortgage went to amass $1.1 million for the mortgage company.

To make matters worse, I'm sure you have been taught that your home is your greatest asset and for this purpose we mean your greatest financial asset. The investment in your home is not just your down payment and mortgage payments, but also the property taxes, the homeowners insurance, and the maintenance to your home. At the end of 30 years, will your home be worth more than $1.1 million?

Make sure you notice the cash surrender and death benefit columns. After 30 years the $1.1 million cash surrender value represents what your home ought to be worth. The death benefit column is what your home ought to be worth to your kids as their inheritance. Notice the death benefit starts out *immediately* at $1.3 million and grows to $2.4 million. These statements reflect the opening premise. IF you purchased a permanent life insurance policy INSTEAD of a home, what should your home be worth after 30 years? We don't choose to live on the street but it does cost money to live inside! Maybe, it is more than you expected.

Principle #21:

When you borrow against your permanent life insurance contract for a purchase, you do not lose your compounding interest.

Next, for our second example, let's consider the purchase of an automobile. If you finance your automobile with a loan from your bank or a loan from the automobile dealership, they will require that you pay back the loan with interest. We will use the same assumptions as we did earlier in the home or life policy example. Remember that the $1,500 per month went to the bank and not to you, so the $1.1 million after 30 years is the bank's funds and you are left with whatever the home is worth on the market.

However, if you entered into a life insurance policy similar to the one illustrated above, you would have access to loans from the life insurance company equal to the cash value of the policy, or the policy limit if lower in the year you seek the funds to purchase the automobile. Remember, this would be an unstructured loan where the insurance company is going to arrange the loan as an interest-only loan. That is the only requirement, and if you have enough collateral capacity in the policy, the interest does not have to be paid since it can be accrued against the values of the contract.

Let's look at what happens when you pay back the loan and when you don't. We are going to use the year 30 values of the above policy as the benchmark, which includes cash value of $1,164,039 and death benefits of $2,457,277 in year 30.

Assume you purchase a $30,000 automobile in year 6 of the policy when you have the collateral capacity of $38,092 from the year before:

Year	Premium	Total Premiums Paid	Cash Value Increase	Cash Value	Death Benefits
5	18,000.00	90,000.00	15,184	38,092	1,352,633

YR	NET OUTLAY	LOAN AMOUNT RECEIVED	LOAN INTEREST DUE	BEGINNING LOAN BALANCE	GROSS CASH VALUE	NET CASH VALUE	GROSS DEATH BENEFIT	NET DEATH BENEFIT
5	18,000	0	0	0	38,092	38,092	1,352,633	1,352,633
6	-12,000*	30,000	1,320	31,320	54,333	22,952	1,361,063	1,329,683
7	18,000	0	1,381	32,762	71,631	38,806	1,370,808	1,337,983
8	18,000	0	1,444	34,269	90,031	55,695	1,381,868	1,347,532
9	18,000	0	1,511	35,847	109,550	73,633	1,394,150	1,358,234
10	18,000	0	1,580	37,496	131,567	93,998	1,412,274	1,374,704
11	18,000	0	1,653	39,222	156,356	117,058	1,435,694	1,396,396
12	18,000	0	1,729	41,027	183,766	142,659	1,464,004	1,422,897
13	18,000	0	1,809	42,916	213,832	170,833	1,496,686	1,453,687
14	18,000	0	1,892	44,891	246,751	201,773	1,533,352	1,488,374
15	18,000	0	1,979	46,957	282,605	235,557	1,573,598	1,526,550
16	18,000	0	2,070	49,118	321,354	272,141	1,617,026	1,567,812
17	18,000	0	2,165	51,379	363,072	311,594	1,663,377	1,611,899
18	18,000	0	2,265	53,744	407,681	353,833	1,712,279	1,658,431
19	18,000	0	2,369	56,217	455,274	398,948	1,763,535	1,707,209
20	18,000	0	2,478	58,805	505,813	446,894	1,816,901	1,757,982
21	18,000	0	2,592	61,511	560,035	498,405	1,874,154	1,812,524
22	18,000	0	2,712	64,342	617,334	552,867	1,933,249	1,868,782
23	18,000	0	2,837	67,303	677,745	610,311	1,994,000	1,926,566
24	18,000	0	2,967	70,401	741,561	671,023	2,056,263	1,985,726
25	18,000	0	3,104	73,641	808,797	735,012	2,119,901	2,046,117
26	18,000	0	3,247	77,031	874,307	797,127	2,184,862	2,107,682
27	18,000	0	3,396	80,576	942,688	861,956	2,251,112	2,170,380
28	18,000	0	3,552	84,285	1,013,785	929,337	2,318,644	2,234,196
29	18,000	0	3,716	88,164	1,087,528	999,193	2,387,323	2,298,988
30	18,000	0	3,887	92,222	1,164,039	1,071,639	2,457,277	2,364,877

This illustration is based on the same policy assumptions discussed earlier.
Hypothetical illustrations should not be used to predict or project investment results.

* You don't put in $18,000 ($1,500 per month) and the insurance company sends you a check for $12,000. Put the two together and purchase the $30,000 car. The life insurance company applies the $18,000 balance of the loan proceeds to your premium due.

There are a number of things you need to take note of:

1. Interest due accrues each year. In this illustration I am assuming that neither the interest nor the principle is paid for the entire length of this unstructured loan.
2. Consequently, the ending loan balance grows each year.
3. The gross cash value has not changed! This is one of the most important things to notice. This indicates that since you have taken an unstructured loan against your life insurance policy, the entire cash value is intact and continuing to compound. You are not using or borrowing your cash value. You are using "other people's money," namely the insurance company's money.
4. Net cash value represents your collateral capacity which is the amount of money your life insurance company will extend to you as a "no-questions-asked" unstructured loan against your policy.
5. The gross death benefit remains intact, just as the gross cash value does.
6. There is a new value illustrated: net death benefit. This value is generated by subtracting the ending loan balance from the gross death benefit. This illustrates how the insurance company is going to collect the loan it has extended to you:

from your eventual death benefits. Bottom line? You have purchased this car from your dead self!

7. Since the compounding of the interest due is less than the compounding of the gross cash value, this illustrates that the policy will not lapse by merely not paying back the loan, indicating that the loan never needs to be paid back. However, policies may lapse if scheduled premiums are not paid. Please note that this illustration shows that premiums are paid throughout the life of the policy.

Now, there is a consequence to taking this loan and not paying it back. Compare these year 30 values with and without this loan:

	Cash value	Death benefits
Without the loan	$1,164,039	$2,457,277
With the loan and not paid back	$1,071,639	$2,364,877

What did the car cost you if you didn't pay back the loan? It cost you $92,400 of retirement spendable assets or net death benefits. This is similar to the discussion of the diamond ring in the chapter on compound interest. But there are two major differences in using the life insurance policy:

1. You are not required to follow a predetermined repayment schedule that you cannot deviate from other than to repay sooner.

2. You did not lose your compounding. Because you secured your loan through the guaranteed collateralization features of your life insurance contract, your gross cash values (not reflective of the loan) did not change and your dividends were granted based on the gross cash value not the net cash value. If there is a "this is why you purchase

a life insurance policy to assist in making major purchases" scenario – this is it!

Before I can move on and illustrate paying back the loan and the interest that the insurance company charges, we need to understand the difference between a "direct recognition" and a "non-direct recognition" of loans outstanding when crediting dividends. Not all insurance companies work the same way. Direct recognition means that your outstanding loan is carved out and receives a reduced dividend from the non-loaned part of your gross cash value that receives the full divided from the insurance company. Non-direct recognition means that the insurance company turns a "blind eye" to the fact that you have a loan outstanding when they grant their dividends to your contract. The best policy is the one with a "non-direct recognition" dividend policy.

What happens when you pay back your loan with interest? Illustrated below is the same policy with the same assumptions as before and the same loan taken in year six, paying interest only (not letting it accrue each year) and then paying back the loan in full in year 10:

YR	NET OUTLAY	LOAN AMOUNT RECEIVED	LOAN INT/PRINC PAID #	ENDING LOAN BALANCE	GROSS CASH VALUE	NET CASH VALUE	GROSS DEATH BENEFIT	NET DEATH BENEFIT
5	18,000	0	0	0	38,092	38,092	1,352,633	1,352,633
6*	-10,680	30,000	1,320	30,000	54,333	24,333	1,361,063	1,331,063
7**	19,320	0	1,320	30,000	71,631	41,631	1,370,808	1,340,808
8**	19,320	0	1,320	30,000	90,031	60,031	1,381,868	1,351,868
9**	19,320	0	1,320	30,000	109,550	79,550	1,394,150	1,364,150
10***	48,000	0	30,000	0	131,567	131,567	1,412,274	1,412,274
11	18,000	0	0	0	156,356	156,356	1,435,694	1,435,694
12	18,000	0	0	0	183,766	183,766	1,464,004	1,464,004
13	18,000	0	0	0	213,832	213,832	1,496,686	1,496,686
14	18,000	0	0	0	246,751	246,751	1,533,352	1,533,352
15	18,000	0	0	0	282,605	282,605	1,573,598	1,573,598
16	18,000	0	0	0	321,354	321,354	1,617,026	1,617,026
17	18,000	0	0	0	363,072	363,072	1,663,377	1,663,377
18	18,000	0	0	0	407,681	407,681	1,712,279	1,712,279
19	18,000	0	0	0	455,274	455,274	1,763,535	1,763,535
20	18,000	0	0	0	505,813	505,813	1,816,901	1,816,901
21	18,000	0	0	0	560,035	560,035	1,874,154	1,874,154
22	18,000	0	0	0	617,334	617,334	1,933,249	1,933,249
23	18,000	0	0	0	677,745	677,745	1,994,000	1,994,000
24	18,000	0	0	0	741,561	741,561	2,056,263	2,056,263
25	18,000	0	0	0	808,797	808,797	2,119,901	2,119,901
26	18,000	0	0	0	874,307	874,307	2,184,862	2,184,862
27	18,000	0	0	0	942,688	942,688	2,251,112	2,251,112
28	18,000	0	0	0	1,013,785	1,013,785	2,318,644	2,318,644
29	18,000	0	0	0	1,087,528	1,087,528	2,387,323	2,387,323
30	18,000	0	0	0	1,164,039	1,164,039	2,457,277	2,457,277

This illustration is based on the same policy assumptions discussed earlier.
Hypothetical illustrations should not be used to predict or project investment results.

* Year 6 net outlay is the regular premium of $18,000, minus the $30,000 loan, minus the loan interest due [$18,000 premium – $30,000 loan + $1,320 interest].

** Years 7, 8, & 9 net outlay is the regular premium plus the interest you pay that year.

*** Year 10 net outlay is the regular premium you pay plus your repayment of the loan principle of $30,000.

Now, there are a number of things you need to take note of:

1. Interest is paid each year. In year 10 the loan principle is repaid (just as an example, in reality, you choose the repayment schedule).
2. Consequently the loan balance stays the same each year.
3. The gross cash value has not changed! This is one of the most important things to notice. You wouldn't expect this since you have just learned that you have taken an unstructured loan *against* your life insurance policy, not *from* your life insurance policy. The entire cash value is intact and continuing to compound. You are not using or borrowing from your cash value. You are using "other people's money," namely the insurance company's money.
4. Net cash value represents your collateral capacity, the amount of money your life insurance company will extend to you as a "no-questions-asked," unstructured loan against your policy. Some insurance companies may limit your maximum loan amount to a percentage of your net cash value.
5. The net cash value and net death benefit in year 10 are exactly what they were in our base line example:

No loan ever taken year 10 (base line):

Year	Premium	Total Premiums	Cash Value Increase	Net Cash Value	Net Death Benefit
10	18,000.00	180,000.00	22,018	131,567	1,412,274

Loan taken in year 6, repaid with interest by year 10:

10	18,000.00	180,000.00	22,018	131,567	1,412,274

6. The gross benefit remains intact, just as the gross cash value does. However, in this example the net death benefit and the net cash value is the same as the gross. Your entire collateral capacity has been restored. Remember, collateral capacity can only be increased by your contributions, growth on your contributions, and the reduction of your loan balances. Your principle, the interest it would have earned, AND the interest that the interest would have earned (the compounding effect) has all been reestablished because you used a life insurance policy to obtain the money you needed for the car. Nowhere else does this happen other than your life insurance policy.

7. Notice the net death benefit. Remember, this value is generated by subtracting the ending loan balance from the gross death benefit. This illustrates how the insurance company is going to collect the loan it has extended to you – from your eventual death benefits. Since the net death benefit has been reestablished to the same level as the gross death benefit there is nothing to collect; the loan has been repaid.

8. It is also important to remember that if policy premiums are not paid when due, a lapse in the policy may take place. In this type of planning, that would be an unacceptable consequence. Remember, too, that dividends projected are the same dividends currently being paid (I am assuming 6%, current dividend rates range from 5% - 7%). Future dividends are not guaranteed.

There is NO consequence to taking this loan when you pay it back. Compare the year 30 values with taking the loan and paying it back and without the loan.

	Cash value	Death benefits
Without the loan	$1,164,039	$2,457,277
With the loan paid back	$1,164,039	$2,457,277

Buying the car with a loan from your insurance company had no negative effect to your retirement savings plan. If there is a "this is why you purchase a life insurance policy to assist in making major purchases and paying those loans back" scenario – this is it!

Ready to take the next step? If you were going to buy one car this way, why wouldn't you buy all your cars this way? How about buying that $30,000 car every other year? Let's see, using all of the same assumptions as before. You'd better be sitting down!

YR	NET OUTLAY	LOAN AMOUNT RECEIVED	LOAN INTEREST DUE	LOAN BALANCE	GROSS CASH VALUE	NET CASH VALUE	GROSS DEATH BENEFIT	NET DEATH BENEFIT
5	18,000	0	0	0	38,092	38,092	1,352,633	1,352,633
6*	-12,000	30,000	1,320	31,320	54,333	22,952	1,361,063	1,329,683
7	18,000	0	1,381	32,762	71,631	38,806	1,370,808	1,337,983
8	-12,000	30,000	2,764	65,589	90,031	24,314	1,381,868	1,316,151
9	18,000	0	2,892	68,608	109,550	40,808	1,394,150	1,325,409
10	-12,000	30,000	4,345	103,086	131,567	28,282	1,412,274	1,308,988
11	18,000	0	4,545	107,830	156,356	48,316	1,435,694	1,327,655
12	-12,000	30,000	6,074	144,113	183,766	39,373	1,464,004	1,319,611
13	18,000	0	6,353	150,746	213,832	62,793	1,496,686	1,345,647
14	-12,000	30,000	7,966	189,004	246,751	57,380	1,533,352	1,343,981
15	18,000	0	8,332	197,703	282,605	84,519	1,573,598	1,375,512
16	-12,000	30,000	10,036	238,122	321,354	82,770	1,617,026	1,378,441
17	18,000	0	10,498	249,082	363,072	113,507	1,663,377	1,413,812
18	-12,000	30,000	12,301	291,866	407,681	115,249	1,712,279	1,419,847
19	18,000	0	12,867	305,299	455,274	149,382	1,763,535	1,457,644
20	-12,000	30,000	14,779	350,671	505,813	154,462	1,816,901	1,465,550
21	18,000	0	15,459	366,810	560,035	192,513	1,874,154	1,506,632
22	-12,000	30,000	17,491	415,013	617,334	201,517	1,933,249	1,517,431
23	18,000	0	18,296	434,114	677,745	242,789	1,994,000	1,559,044
24	-12,000	30,000	20,458	485,414	741,561	255,205	2,056,263	1,569,908
25	18,000	0	21,400	507,755	808,797	300,057	2,119,901	1,611,161
26	-12,000	30,000	23,705	562,445	874,307	310,771	2,184,862	1,621,327
27	18,000	0	24,796	588,331	942,688	353,216	2,251,112	1,661,640
28	-12,000	30,000	27,257	646,729	1,013,785	365,802	2,318,644	1,670,661
29	18,000	0	28,511	676,495	1,087,528	409,721	2,387,323	1,709,515
30	-12,000	30,000	31,144	738,951	1,164,039	423,655	2,457,277	1,716,893
31**	17,543	0	32,577	772,961	1,243,476	469,016	2,528,620	1,754,159
32	-12,457	30,000	35,396	839,857	1,326,072	484,586	2,601,433	1,759,948
33	17,543	0	37,025	878,511	1,412,127	531,912	2,675,857	1,795,642
34	-12,457	30,000	40,049	950,265	1,501,776	549,668	2,751,944	1,799,836
35	17,543	0	41,893	994,001	1,595,997	600,068	2,830,965	1,835,036
36	-12,457	30,000	45,141	1,071,070	1,694,962	621,814	2,913,332	1,840,184
37	17,543	0	47,218	1,120,366	1,798,870	676,331	2,999,251	1,876,712
38	-12,457	30,000	50,712	1,203,251	1,907,449	701,864	3,089,034	1,883,450
39	17,543	0	53,046	1,258,631	2,021,114	760,042	3,183,051	1,921,979
40	-12,457	30,000	56,807	1,347,879	2,140,475	789,982	3,281,727	1,931,233
41	17,543	0	59,422	1,409,915	2,265,914	853,263	3,385,401	1,972,750
42	-12,457	30,000	63,477	1,506,127	2,397,870	888,821	3,494,461	1,985,412
43	17,543	0	66,398	1,575,447	2,536,523	958,021	3,609,336	2,030,834
44	-12,457	30,000	70,774	1,679,277	2,681,983	999,449	3,730,478	2,047,944
45	17,543	0	74,032	1,756,566	2,834,319	1,074,346	3,858,325	2,098,352
46	-12,457	30,000	78,759	1,868,732	2,993,875	1,121,518	3,993,313	2,120,956

This illustration is based on the same policy assumptions discussed earlier.

Hypothetical illustrations should not be used to predict or project investment results.

* Year 6 and every even year thereafter – You don't put in your premium ($18,000) it is instead borrowed against the policy and your insurance company sends you

$12,000. Put the two together and purchase a $30,000 automobile. (ie: the premium you would have paid plus net proceeds from the policy loan)

** Year 31 – this happens to be the year that the 35-year-old (with all of the premium assumptions as previously discussed) in this illustration turns 65. At the origination of the contract, he arranged for a special rider to be added to his life insurance policy. He added a "waiver of premium for disability" rider. At age 65 this rider expires, so there is no longer a part of the premium that is set aside to offset the cost of this rider. Consequently, the premium deposit is reduced. This rider, upon permanent disability, continues the premium deposits for him. Be careful: you want an insurance company that will add the premium to the policy, not one who merely waives the premium. A waived premium merely dismisses the future premiums and all that is left to grow is your money and what it has earned. Not bad, but not good enough. You want an insurance company who will continue deposits. An insurance company who continues the deposits ensures that you can purchase that automobile every 2 years, or perhaps you might think of another use of $30,000 every two years. You can't do this with an insurance company who merely waives the premium.

There are a number of things you need to take note of:

1. Interest accrues each year. In this illustration I am assuming that neither the interest nor the principle of any of the loans is paid for the entire length of this unstructured loan.
2. Consequently, the ending loan balance grows each year.
3. The gross cash value has not changed from the original base line illustration! This is one of the

most important things to notice. This indicates that since you have taken an unstructured loan against your life insurance policy, the entire cash value is intact and continuing to compound. You are not using or borrowing your cash value. You are using "other people's money," namely the insurance company's money.

4. Net cash value represents your collateral capacity: the amount of money your life insurance company will extend to you as a "no-questions-asked," unstructured loan against your policy. Because you are adding $18,000 to it each year, it is increasing every other year. Because of uninterrupted compounding of your gross cash value, the net cash value goes up **every** year; even in a year you buy another car.

5. The gross death benefit remains intact, just as the gross cash value does.

6. Look at the net death benefit. This value is generated by subtracting the ending loan balance from the gross death benefit. This illustrates how the insurance company is going to collect the loan it has extended to you – from your eventual death benefits. Bottom line? You have purchased all your cars from your dead self!

7. Since the compounding of the interest due is less than the compounding of the gross cash value, this policy illustrates that the policy will not lapse, indicating that the loans never need to be paid back. However, remember policies may lapse if scheduled premiums are not paid, resulting in unacceptable consequences.

There is a consequence to taking this loan and not paying it back. Compare these year 30 values with and without this loan:

	Cash value	Death benefits
Without the loan	$1,164,039	$2,457,277
With the loan and not paid back	$ 423,655	$1,716,893

What did the car cost you if you don't pay back the loans? It costs you $740,384 of retirement spendable assets or net death benefits. Don't forget, during that time you have also purchased thirteen $30,000 cars. Do you really care?

Think about it this way: what if you purchased these $30,000 cars the old fashioned way? Save/spend, save/spend, save/spend. What would you have at the end of 30 years? You would have:

1. About $210,000 in the bank, if you could earn a 5% return on your money. That is only true if you paid the taxes due on the growth of that money from some other account. Remember, you would be saving $18,000 every year and taking out $30,000 every other year. A net savings of $6,000 every other year at 5% is about $210,000.
2. A new car.

Review what you would have if you made these purchases against your life insurance policy. You would have:

1. About $423,000 in the net cash value of your life insurance policy available to you without having to pay income taxes.
2. A new car.

3. Protection for your family with anywhere from $1,300,000 to $1,700,000 in the event of your premature death.

4. This insurance plan in place whether or not you became disabled.

That is $213,000 more than the generally accepted method of save/spend, save/spend, save/spend. What would you do with an extra $213,000 at retirement? What would your family do with an extra $1,300,000 if you didn't live to see retirement?

Let's keep going because life does not end at age 65. You have two choices: you can either begin to supplement your other retirement income with $423,000, or you could keep buying cars.

Let's buy cars, and we will discuss the retirement income in the next chapter:

Assuming you keep buying cars until you are 80 years old (the kids take the keys away at 82) and you live to your life expectancy of 84. At age 80, you will have purchased another eight $30,000 cars for a total of twenty-one cars over your lifetime. Referring to the most recent illustration in this chapter, at age 80 your net cash values are over $1,100,000 (year 46 in the illustration):

YR	LOAN AMOUNT RECEIVED *	LOAN INTEREST DUE	LOAN BALANCE	GROSS CASH VALUE	NET CASH VALUE	GROSS DEATH BENEFIT	NET DEATH BENEFIT
46	30,000	78,759	1,868,732	2,993,875	1,121,518	3,993,313	2,120,956

Sounds like a long-term care solution just because you saved as much as you were putting toward your home mortgage and you purchased your vehicles a different way. If you don't need the long-term care solution, you would be leaving your beneficiaries over $2,100,000 when you leave this world. Now that is a legacy! All because you were financially responsible and learned the truth about life insurance.

However, if you stop buying cars and instead choose to use the net cash value to enhance your retirement stream of income, $423,000 is still not enough to retire on. Remember how this chapter began:

"The secret of wealth accumulation is this: whenever you relieve yourself of a regular expenditure - whether it be some ongoing expense or a debt repayment stream of cash that has satisfied the debt - continue making those payments, but to yourself. The car payments fit in your budget for 36 months, so keep it in your budget, but pay it to yourself. If you don't, you will find other ways to spend it in ways you don't even realize."

Principle #22:

Start a new permanent life insurance policy every time you pay off a loan or eliminate a recurring expenditure.

Let's say that you normally pay off your car loans every 5 years. On a $30,000 loan, that would be $6,000 per year. Remember, you are buying a car every 2 years in the examples of this chapter, but let's assume you are only tackling the repayment of every third car purchased. That means that every five years you will have freed up a car payment of $6,000 per year. If the secret of wealth accumulation is to continue spending even when the debt is satisfied, that means you could start a new insurance policy with $6,000 per year every 5 years. How would this look?

- Age 35 – start the plan.
- Age 40 – add your second policy, at $6,000 per year, perhaps this time insuring your spouse. After all, you both want to sleep well at night.
- Age 45 – add a third policy.
- Age 50 – add a fourth policy.
- Age 55 – add a fifth policy.

We will stop there, because the design of these policies may be a bit different. I'd prefer to limit the funding period to age 65, since that is my expected date of retirement. At retirement, I will begin to reverse the funding and actually take money out of the policies. WAIT – if you have understood up to this point, you should be saying, "I don't want to take money out of my policies, I'd rather take loans against my policies, right?" RIGHT.

Let's see how much accumulates in each of these additional policies. Again, I'm assuming good health and all of the original assumptions each time you apply for a new policy:

Policy #	Premium Paid	Cash Value at age 65	Death Benefit at age 65
2 – taken at age 40	$150,000	$236,000	$439,000
3 – taken at age 45	$120,000	$156,000	$291,000
4 – taken at age 50	$90,000	$100,000	$187,000
5 – taken at age 55	$60,000	$60,000	$114,000
TOTAL	$420,000	$552,000	$1,031,000

You have accumulated over half a million dollars available to you income tax-free, and just because you learned the secret of accumulating wealth.

Chapter 12

Retirement Income Alternatives

Principle #23:

Permanent life insurance during retirement gives you
cash flow options not otherwise advisable.

When it comes time to generate a retirement cash flow,
you can do one of two things with your life insurance policies.

First, you could merely begin a series of systematic loans
against your life policies. Let's look at the original policy that
you funded with the same cash flow as the mortgage on your
house: $1,500 per month. All the same assumptions as
before, a healthy 35-year-old.

YR	TOTAL ANNUALIZED PREMIUM	CUMULATIVE NET ANNUALIZED OUTLAY	CASH VALUE INCREASE	TOTAL CASH SURRENDER VALUE	TOTAL DEATH BENEFIT
1	18,000.00	18,000.00	13	13	1,334,407
2	18,000.00	36,000.00	401	414	1,336,234
3	18,000.00	54,000.00	8,311	8,726	1,340,098
4	18,000.00	72,000.00	14,183	22,908	1,345,625
5	18,000.00	90,000.00	15,184	38,092	1,352,633
6	18,000.00	108,000.00	16,240	54,333	1,361,063
7	18,000.00	126,000.00	17,299	71,631	1,370,808
8	18,000.00	144,000.00	18,399	90,031	1,381,868
9	18,000.00	162,000.00	19,519	109,550	1,394,150
10	18,000.00	180,000.00	22,018	131,567	1,412,274
11	18,000.00	198,000.00	24,789	156,356	1,435,694
12	18,000.00	216,000.00	27,410	183,766	1,464,004
13	18,000.00	234,000.00	30,066	213,832	1,496,686
14	18,000.00	252,000.00	32,919	246,751	1,533,352
15	18,000.00	270,000.00	35,855	282,605	1,573,598
16	18,000.00	288,000.00	38,749	321,354	1,617,026
17	18,000.00	306,000.00	41,718	363,072	1,663,377
18	18,000.00	324,000.00	44,609	407,681	1,712,279
19	18,000.00	342,000.00	47,593	455,274	1,763,535
20	18,000.00	360,000.00	50,539	505,813	1,816,901
21	18,000.00	378,000.00	54,222	560,035	1,874,154
22	18,000.00	396,000.00	57,299	617,334	1,933,249
23	18,000.00	414,000.00	60,411	677,745	1,994,000
24	18,000.00	432,000.00	63,816	741,561	2,056,263
25	18,000.00	450,000.00	67,236	808,797	2,119,901
26	18,000.00	468,000.00	65,510	874,307	2,184,862
27	18,000.00	486,000.00	68,381	942,688	2,251,112
28	18,000.00	504,000.00	71,097	1,013,785	2,318,644
29	18,000.00	522,000.00	73,743	1,087,528	2,387,323
30	18,000.00	540,000.00	76,511	1,164,039	2,457,277

This illustration is based on the same policy assumptions discussed earlier.
Hypothetical illustrations should not be used to predict or project investment results.

Remember, these are the same year 30 values when you used this policy as collateral to finance major expenses during your working life as long as you paid them back each time. If you did not pay back the loans, your collateral capacity will be diminished and the following flow of retirement cash will not be available.

If you paid back all the loans, at age 65 you would have $1,164,039 of collateral capacity to borrow retirement funds against a death benefit of $2,457,277. You could enjoy a retirement cash flow of 88,473 per year if you chose to take level loans against this life policy for 20 years (to age 85). If this was your only source of retirement cash flow in addition to social security, you may be eligible for things like food stamps depending on what the government requirements would be for public assistance at the time of your retirement. Because this retirement cash flow is not reported on any tax form, your social security payments would not be subject to tax either. If this were a retirement "income" subject to income taxes, 85% of your social security payments would be taxable at whatever rate is in effect that year. This additional tax on social security will be at your marginal rate, the highest rate applicable to any of your income that year.

The following is the chart showing the retirement cash flow from the life insurance policy:

AGE	NET OUTLAY	LOAN AMOUNT RECEIVED	LOAN INTEREST DUE	ENDING LOAN BALANCE	GROSS CASH VALUE	NET CASH VALUE	GROSS DEATH BENEFIT	NET DEATH BENEFIT
65	18,000	0	0	0	1,164,039	1,164,039	2,457,277	2,457,277
66	-88,473	88,473	3,893	92,545	1,225,618	1,133,073	2,496,294	2,403,749
67	-88,473	88,473	7,965	189,349	1,289,354	1,100,004	2,536,654	2,347,304
68	-88,473	88,473	12,224	290,609	1,355,492	1,064,882	2,578,436	2,287,826
69	-88,473	88,473	16,680	396,529	1,424,114	1,027,585	2,621,644	2,225,114
70	-88,473	88,473	21,340	507,325	1,496,139	988,814	2,667,496	2,160,171
71	-88,473	88,473	26,215	623,219	1,571,685	948,466	2,716,344	2,093,125
72	-88,473	88,473	31,314	744,448	1,650,895	906,447	2,768,333	2,023,884
73	-88,473	88,473	36,649	871,256	1,733,473	862,216	2,823,698	1,952,441
74	-88,473	88,473	42,228	1,003,901	1,819,763	815,862	2,882,720	1,878,819
75	-88,473	88,473	48,064	1,142,651	1,910,280	767,629	2,945,729	1,803,078
76	-88,473	88,473	54,169	1,287,786	2,005,325	717,538	3,012,971	1,725,185
77	-88,473	88,473	60,555	1,439,602	2,105,242	665,641	3,084,733	1,645,132
78	-88,473	88,473	67,235	1,598,405	2,210,145	611,740	3,161,334	1,562,930
79	-88,473	88,473	74,223	1,764,516	2,320,087	555,571	3,243,115	1,478,599
80	-88,473	88,473	81,532	1,938,273	2,435,082	496,808	3,330,386	1,392,113
81	-88,473	88,473	89,177	2,120,027	2,555,389	435,362	3,423,459	1,303,431
82	-88,473	88,473	97,174	2,310,147	2,681,172	371,025	3,522,785	1,212,638
83	-88,473	88,473	105,539	2,509,017	2,813,039	304,022	3,628,724	1,119,707
84	-88,473	88,473	114,290	2,717,039	2,951,516	234,476	3,741,699	1,024,660
85	-88,473	88,473	123,443	2,934,636	3,097,040	162,404	3,862,330	927,693
86	0	0	129,124	3,069,703	3,249,873	180,170	3,991,230	921,527
87	0	0	135,067	3,210,987	3,410,481	199,495	4,129,175	918,189
88	0	0	141,283	3,358,773	3,579,416	220,643	4,277,127	918,354
89	0	0	147,786	3,513,361	3,757,445	244,084	4,436,099	922,738
90	0	0	154,588	3,675,063	3,941,640	266,576	4,602,768	927,704
91	0	0	161,703	3,844,209	4,129,919	285,710	4,774,948	930,739
92	0	0	169,145	4,021,139	4,322,171	301,032	4,951,132	929,993
93	0	0	176,930	4,206,212	4,517,599	311,387	5,130,440	924,228
94	0	0	185,073	4,399,803	4,715,588	315,784	5,312,350	912,546
95	0	0	193,591	4,602,305	4,915,666	313,361	5,496,634	894,329
96	0	0	202,501	4,814,126	5,117,467	303,341	5,683,212	869,085
97	0	0	211,822	5,035,697	5,322,649	286,952	5,871,889	836,192
98	0	0	221,571	5,267,466	5,531,126	263,661	6,062,445	794,979
99	0	0	231,768	5,509,901	5,743,183	233,281	6,254,633	744,732
100	0	0	242,436	5,763,495	5,959,478	195,983	6,448,256	684,761

This illustration is based on the same policy assumptions discussed earlier.
Hypothetical illustrations should not be used to predict or project investment results.

Now, let's go through each column and describe what is going on:

Age: your age, remembering that this policy was started at age 35 and illustrated for 30 years to get the age 65 values. These are the same cash value and death benefits at age 65 you have seen in previous chapters.

Net Outlay: notice the last premium payment (money from you) is made at age 65 and the first cash flow distribution (money to you) is at age 66.

Loan Amount Received: the cash to you is coming in the form of a loan from the insurance company (using your cash value as collateral).

Loan Interest Due: this is a loan from the insurance company, so they are going to want to collect interest on the loan. If you don't pay it, a lien is placed against the policy increasing the lien against the death benefit, which will be collected at your death.

Ending Loan Balance: it is assumed that you are not paying back the loan or the interest due, so the loan balance grows each year.

Gross Cash Value – your gross cash value is your premiums and dividend credits with uninterrupted compounding. It is this value that is used to determine your dividend credit each year.

Net Cash Value – this is your collateral capacity, or the amount of future loans and/or interest that can be borrowed against the policy.

Gross Death Benefit – this is a fairly meaningless number. It merely shows what the benefit to your beneficiaries would be if you pay back all of the outstanding loans and interest accrued on the day before you die.

Net Death Benefit – this is what your beneficiaries would receive. This is what is left after the insurance company has reclaimed its loans to you with interest.

Notice that this example illustrates out to age 100. The illustration is shown at current dividend (6%, current dividend rates range from 5% - 7%) and loan interest rates (4.4%). Your use of the policy should be carefully reviewed each year. The insurance policy shown is an example of a fairly standard policy. It is assumed to be a policy from a company that uses the non-direct recognition rule when it comes to crediting dividends, and this can make a big difference. This difference can be mitigated with the proper policy design. Some insurance companies provide a way to link the dividend rate and the loan interest rate. If this is possible, it serves a great advantage because the dividend credited on gross cash value (the bigger number) uses the same rate as the cost of the outstanding loan (the smaller number). The dividends assumed are not guaranteed and may result in the policy projecting to something considerably less than age 100.

Principle #24:

The most important asset to own at retirement is a permanent life insurance contract where the death benefit is equal to the amount of your other assets.

The second way you can use your life insurance as a retirement income tool is to leverage the death benefits against other retirement assets. This discussion will assume that by the time you reach retirement age you will have saved $2.5 million dollars in other retirement accounts by age 65. If this is an unimaginable large number for you, be aware that this discussion is scalable. If you are able to save $1.25 million dollars, then cut the numbers that follow in half. If you only have $625,000, then divide by 4. If you can save $5 million dollars then double everything. Few people save enough money for retirement.

The reason I am using the example of $2.5 million dollars of other retirement accounts is because the most important asset to have in retirement is a permanent life insurance policy whose death benefit is equal to one times the retirement assets available during retirement. The reason a permanent life insurance policy is so important is because it allows you to live not only on the interest your nest egg can provide, but you can also spend the principle. You can spend the principle because you know that at some date in the future all the retirement assets you and your spouse spend during a retirement lifetime together will be replaced by the death benefit, and then ready to be spent again by the surviving spouse. Let's see how this works out.

The traditional financial planning approach is to use 4% as the "safe" distribution rate from your nest egg. The theory indicates that your portfolio ought to be able to earn 4%, therefore living on the interest not only means you won't run out of a retirement cash flow, but you will also leave the nest egg behind as a legacy to your beneficiaries. However, during the period from 2008 through 2013 (the time this book was being written), retirees were hard-pressed to earn anywhere near 4% safely, forcing them into a reduced cash flow and dangerously dipping into their principle or entering the equities market and subjecting their nest egg to market risks.

Not only has the 4% withdrawal "rule" had to survive recent low interest rates and market volatility, the rule has also been challenged by:

1. Inflation – 4% of a fixed "nest egg" results in a fixed cash flow. A fixed cash flow is stressed by the cost of general goods and services going up each year. $40,000 (the cash flow generated by a $1,000,000 nest egg) will purchase more in your first year of retirement than 20 years later. Either you will need to eliminate something you want to purchase or you will dip into the nest egg which will diminish future cash flows or hasten the day the nest egg will run out.

2. Taxes – if 4% represents the growth of the nest egg, it also represents income taxable from an investment such as a CD. That will result in $40,000 (the cash flow generated by a $1,000,000 nest egg) of taxable income. If taxes go up during your retirement years that will put the same pressure on choosing what not to purchase the next year or begin a reduction of the nest egg to pay the increased taxes.

3. Non-Budgeted Expenditures – in the 4% model, every future purchase must fit in the 4% budget. Any expenditure over and above what the nest egg generates each year will either have to be financed by going into debt or you will again need to dip into the nest egg.

Any reduction of principle (nest egg) may result in your money running out before you run out of life!

Running out of money in retirement is as serious as a premature death. When planning your retirement cash flows, just make sure that you are comfortable with your probability of success. If your probability of not running out of money by the time you reached your life expectancy is 95% would you go forward with the plan?

What is the probability that you will live beyond age 85?

According to data compiled by the Social Security Administration:

- A man reaching age 65 today can expect to live, on average, until age 84.
- A woman turning age 65 today can expect to live, on average, until age 86.

And those are just averages. About one out of every four 65-year-olds today will live past age 90, and one out of 10 will live past age 95 (http://www.ssa.gov/planners/lifeexpectancy.htm).

More importantly, what is the probability that one of two marriage partners will live beyond age 85? After all, the retirement nest egg must last as long as the last marriage partner survives. For two 65 year olds, their joint expectancy is 91. Therefore, it is prudent to simulate the probability of financial success well past age 85 (http://www.nyc.gov/html/olr/downloads/pdf/nyceira/joint_table.pdf).

The best rate of success if you wanted your nest egg to last to age 100 is 84%. That sounds good, but let me put it a different way.

What if you have just celebrated your retirement by spending two weeks on an African safari (or fill in whatever your dream vacation may be)? You are now on the last leg of your trip home, the flight from London to New York or wherever you call home. As you are waiting for your plane to board, you notice the pilots standing near the boarding door waiting to board the plane themselves. If you were to engage them in a conversation about the probability of landing safely in New York and they described the weather in both London and New York and the conditions flying over the Atlantic and they concluded that there was an 84% chance of landing safely, would you get on the plane? I wouldn't! Yet, that is exactly what traditional financial planning is asking retirees to do every day as they explain the 4% withdrawal theory. By the way, I wouldn't get on the plane with a 95% chance of a safe landing either.

Can we do better? Yes, we can. And it is accomplished by owning a life insurance policy whose death benefit is equal to one times your assets at retirement.

What I didn't say was that the only asset you own is permanent life insurance. However, as illustrated in the previous chapter, that would work as well. But most people come into financial planning with some assets already accumulated.

In this chapter, I am going to use a hypothetical example based on data from a married couple with two children I recently met. Let's call them Jacob and Sandy. They currently have traditional qualified plan retirement assets of $500,000, and 529 plans for each of their two daughters. They are funding their 401(k) plan with $17,000 per year and the 529 plans with $6,000 each per year. Their total cash flow for education and retirement is $29,000 per year. They wanted to know if they could do better. They are ages 41 and 47.

Assuming that the 529 savings would take care of college, we focused on their qualified plans. If their 401(k) were to grow at 6% each year without adding any more money, in 24 years when the youngest reaches age 65 the qualified plans would have $2 million dollars. If they had continued to add $17,000 per year to the plan the nest egg would be $2.9 million dollars.

Using the traditional 4% withdrawal theory, which doesn't work 100% of the time, they would either have $80,000 of taxable income in retirement or $116,000 of taxable income. If they restrict themselves to only consuming 4% - assuming they can earn 4% each year - they should never run out of money and leave the entire nest egg for their beneficiaries.

Notice this is taxable income. It is taxable for two reasons. First, it represents earnings on the investments, which are always taxable whether this is a qualified plan or not. Second, since it is qualified plan money, it is always 100% taxable at whatever the ordinary income tax rates are in the year of distribution because income tax deductions were taken each year on the $17,000 put into the qualified plan each year. Reducing these cash flows for taxes of a combined federal and state rate of 25%, the $80,000 cash flow has been reduced to $60,000 and the $116,000 cash flow has been reduced to $87,000. I'm picking a combined rate of 25% because I believe it is a conservative rate since the future pressure is for taxes to go up. This is not accounting for the taxes due on social security that either of these two taxable cash flows would require by the IRS.

Let's look at the pressures put on this traditional approach to retirement income planning:

1. Inflation: both cash flows are fixed cash flows if inflation requires a larger distribution to cover the cost of your standard of living. You are either

going to have to reduce your standard of living so you don't invade the principle, or you are going to have to withdraw some of the principle. This means you won't have as much invested the next year earning 4%. If you don't have as much earning 4% the next year, you will need to withdraw less the next year and EVERY year thereafter. Inflation occurs every year of our lives so it is unreasonable to think that in retirement you will be exempt from inflation.

2. Taxes: we are assuming that taxes will remain at this 25% combined level. How realistic is that? If tax rates go up in your retirement years, your spendable income will go down. Some people believe that in retirement you don't pay taxes anymore; while others believe that at some certain age, taxes are eliminated. For some of you, you know better, but I have run into enough surprised people who are amazed that they even have to file a tax return in retirement. And this is why it needs to be mentioned here. If you don't believe that the taxes you are going to be paying in the future are going to increase, please ask yourself the following questions:

   a. Where do you think we are going to get the money to "shore up" Social Security? We have been told that Social Security needs to be shored up. Right now, your social security statement has some qualifying language. Currently the sample social security statement shown on the Social Security website says this: "Your estimated benefits are based on current law. Congress has made changes to the law in the past and can do so at any time. The law governing benefit amounts may change because, by 2033, the payroll taxes collected will be enough to pay only about 77 percent of scheduled benefits" (www.ssa.gov).

b. We have been told that Medicare needs to be bailed out. Where will that money come from?

c. We are in the midst of a continuing fight against terrorism, whether you call it a war on terrorism or not. Where will the money come from to defend our national borders?

d. The federal deficit is $17 trillion dollars. (http://www.usdebtclock.org) Every plan to reduce the federal deficit involves increasing taxes. Need I say more?

3. Interest Rates: what if you can't earn 4%. Have you been earning 4% on your safe money these last few years?

4. Market Risk: if you can't earn 4%, or you just believe you can do better in the market, you may choose or be forced to take market risks with your money. Can your nest egg withstand a 40% decline as growth mutual funds did in 2008? If your $2 million dollar nest egg suffers a 40% loss, that means you have to earn more than 6.5% each and EVERY year thereafter to continue the same retirement cash flow.

5. Spending Risk: you might just want something that doesn't fit into your current cash flow budget. What if that want became a "need?" You worked your entire life to get out of debt so you could live your retirement debt free and now you are faced with going back into debt or dipping into your nest egg.

Now consider what is possible if Jacob and Sandy embrace the premise that "permanent life insurance is the most important asset to own in retirement."

If Jacob and Sandy own life insurance equal to or close to the value of their retirement nest egg, then they don't have to live on interest alone. They can plan to live on interest AND principle in their retirement.

Normal life expectancy is around 85; if we choose that age as our planning objective then that is 20 years of necessary retirement cash flow. The "interest only" approach only works 84-95% of the time if all of the risks previously listed are eliminated. The perfect "interest only" plan would also leave the nest egg as a legacy to beneficiaries.

Using the principle and interest approach, planning on completely draining the qualified plan at age 85 would give Jacob and Sandy a gross withdrawal of $147,164 instead of $80,000 (assuming the same 4% rate of growth). After taxes, that is annual spendable cash flow of $110,373 instead of $60,000. That is 84% more spendable cash flow than the interest only approach. You would only attempt to do this if you knew with certainty that at some point in time the principle would be replaced by the death benefits of the life insurance policy.

For my analytical readers, the following diagram compares conserving principle and consuming principle:

Age	Con–serve Gross Withdr awal	Con–serve Tax Rate Per–centage	Con–serve Taxes Paid	Conserve Pur–chasing Power	Cons–ume Gross With–drawal	Cons–ume Tax Rate Percenta ge	Consu me Taxes Paid	Con–sume Pur–chasing Power	Per–centage More
65	80,000	25%	-20,000	60,000	147,164	25%	-36,791	110,373	84%
66	80,000	25%	-20,000	60,000	147,164	25%	-36,791	110,373	84%
67	80,000	25%	-20,000	60,000	147,164	25%	-36,791	110,373	84%
68	80,000	25%	-20,000	60,000	147,164	25%	-36,791	110,373	84%
69	80,000	25%	-20,000	60,000	147,164	25%	-36,791	110,373	84%
70	80,000	25%	-20,000	60,000	147,164	25%	-36,791	110,373	84%
71	80,000	25%	-20,000	60,000	147,164	25%	-36,791	110,373	84%
72	80,000	25%	-20,000	60,000	147,164	25%	-36,791	110,373	84%
73	80,000	25%	-20,000	60,000	147,164	25%	-36,791	110,373	84%
74	80,000	25%	-20,000	60,000	147,164	25%	-36,791	110,373	84%
75	80,000	25%	-20,000	60,000	147,164	25%	-36,791	110,373	84%
76	80,000	25%	-20,000	60,000	147,164	25%	-36,791	110,373	84%
77	80,000	25%	-20,000	60,000	147,164	25%	-36,791	110,373	84%
78	80,000	25%	-20,000	60,000	147,164	25%	-36,791	110,373	84%
79	80,000	25%	-20,000	60,000	147,164	25%	-36,791	110,373	84%
80	80,000	25%	-20,000	60,000	147,164	25%	-36,791	110,373	84%
81	80,000	25%	-20,000	60,000	147,164	25%	-36,791	110,373	84%
82	80,000	25%	-20,000	60,000	147,164	25%	-36,791	110,373	84%
83	80,000	25%	-20,000	60,000	147,164	25%	-36,791	110,373	84%
84	80,000	25%	-20,000	60,000	147,164	25%	-36,791	110,373	84%

Remaining Balance: $2,000,000   Remaining Balance: $0

To recap, in this illustration there were not any new contributions to the 401(k) and the assets were invested to earn at 6% until retirement age of 65. The money, otherwise added to the 401(k) and education savings, was instead used to purchase the life insurance policy.

There are a number of questions that you should be asking.

1. What if I live past 85; what will I live on then?
2. What about saving for and sending the kids to college?
3. What if the new money was still flowing into the 401(k) plan and you didn't buy the life insurance?
4. What if this isn't qualified plan (401(k)) money?

Let's address each question:

Question #1 is answered by drawing your attention to the cash surrender value of the life insurance policy that has not been paid out since you didn't die. Because Jacob and Sandy have been consuming their retirement plan balance for the last 20 years, that has left the compounding that has been occurring in their life insurance contract untouched. Remember that permanent life insurance is an asset that grows tax-deferred, so no taxes have ever been paid on the compounding growth during this entire 20-year period in retirement.

Looking at the cash value of the permanent life insurance policy that has now been compounding for 44 years, at 2013 dividend rates (24 years before retirement and 20 years after) without adding new premiums to the contract during the retirement years, the cash value of the contract is almost $2 million, an amount that approximates the initial retirement plan nest egg. So live or die, the life insurance contract replaces the spent nest egg just at the right time.

Before I show you the spend-down of the life insurance cash value after age 85 (which is where you turn for money when the retirement nest egg has been depleted), let's address question #2. What about saving for and sending the kids to college? What I have yet to disclose to you is that the $2 million cash value at age 85 is after borrowing $20,000 per year for four years for each of the two children to go to college against the same life insurance contract. Inherent in Jacob and Sandy's planning, college education is going to cost $80,000 per child, rendering the 529 plan savings unnecessary if what otherwise was saved for college is redirected toward the permanent life insurance premiums.

There are a few advantages to saving for college while you are also saving for retirement in a life insurance contract:

1. The cash value (equity value) of your life insurance contract is not a reportable asset on the Free Application for Federal Student Aid, a.k.a. FAFSA (www.finaid.org).
2. 529 Education Savings Plans must be used for qualified education expenses. Who defines what is a qualified education expense? The Government!
3. 529 Education Savings Plans must be reported as an asset on the FAFSA form (www.savingforcollege.com).
4. SavingforCollege.com also says this: "sound complicated? It is. And we are only talking about the federal financial aid rules here -- each school can (and most will) set its own rules when handing out its own need-based scholarships, and *many schools are starting to adjust awards when they discover 529 accounts in the family*" (emphasis

added). Also consider that the federal financial aid rules are subject to frequent change. Finally, most financial aid comes in the form of loans, not grants, and so you end up paying it back anyway.

5. The Hope Scholarship and Lifetime Learning tax credits can be claimed in the same year that you take a tax-exempt distribution from a section 529 plan, but the distribution may not be used for the same qualified higher education expenses (www.finaid.org). So, if you want the tax credit, you can't use the 529 plan for those expenses. In all reality, saving for your children's higher education in a 529 plan not only requires a higher education degree for yourself to understand the rules, but it also robs you of your tuition tax credits when you file your income tax return.

6. Whatever 529 plan savings are left when your last child graduates must be given away to a "qualifying family member" in order to preserve the tax-free benefits that you started the plan for in the first place. Guess who decides who a qualifying family member is? Yes, that is right, the Government again. If the money is not given away, it can be used as a retirement asset for yourself, but taxable. You lose all the tax-free benefits you thought you were signing up for. And, you'd better not use it too quickly, or you may also be subject to a 10% penalty in addition to the taxes due.

To be fair, the top seven advantages of using a 529 plan to save for college as cited by http://savingforcollege.com/intro_to_529s/name-the-top-7-benefits-of-529-plans.php are:

1. 529 plans offer unsurpassed income tax breaks. Although your contributions are not deductible on your federal tax return, your investment grows tax-deferred, and distributions to pay for the beneficiary's college costs come out federally tax-free.

2. Your own state may offer some tax breaks as well, like an upfront deduction for your contributions or income exemption on withdrawals, in addition to the federal treatment.

3. You, the donor, stay in control of the account. With few exceptions, the named beneficiary has no rights to the funds. You are the one who calls the shots; you decide when withdrawals are taken and for what purpose.

4. A 529 plan can provide a very easy hands-off way to save for college. Once you decide which 529 plan to use, you complete a simple enrollment form and make your contribution. Then you can relax and forget about it if you like. The ongoing investment of your account is handled by the plan, not by you. Plan assets are professionally managed either by the state treasurer's office or by an outside investment company hired as the program manager.

5. You won't receive a Form 1099 to report taxable or nontaxable earnings until the year you make withdrawals.

6. If you want to move your investment around, you may change to a different option in a 529 savings program every year (program permitting) or you may rollover your account to a different state's program provided no such rollover for your beneficiary has occurred in the prior 12 months.

7. Everyone is eligible to take advantage of a 529 plan, and the amounts you can put in are substantial (over $300,000 per beneficiary in many state plans). Generally, there are no income limitations or age restrictions.

Now, let's look at the loans borrowed against the life insurance contract to fund college **and** to fund retirement after all of the other retirement assets have been consumed. The $29,000 premium comes from the $17,000 otherwise being saved in the 401(k) plan and $6,000 per year for each of the children's 529 plans.

The following illustration assumes the following:

- 41 year old healthy father of 2
- A Whole Life Insurance policy beginning with a death benefit of $787,015 with an annual recurring premium of $29,000.
- Current dividend rates range from 5% - 7%. I am assuming a 6% dividend rate and assume that rate to not change throughout the life of the policy. Future dividends are not guaranteed.

END OF YR AGE	NET OUTLAY	LOAN AMOUNT RECEIVED	ENDING LOAN BALANCE	GROSS CASH VALUE	NET CASH VALUE	GROSS DEATH BENEFIT	NET DEATH BENEFIT
42	29,000	0	0	9,531	9,531	823,528	823,528
43	29,000	0	0	26,998	26,998	861,020	861,020
44	29,000	0	0	50,619	50,619	899,531	899,531
45	29,000	0	0	75,646	75,646	939,045	939,045
46	29,000	0	0	102,180	102,180	979,735	979,735
47	9,000	20,000	20,921	137,097	116,177	1,021,603	1,000,683
College Expenses →		20,000	42,804	174,025	131,221	1,064,725	1,021,921
		40,000	86,615	213,224	126,609	1,109,278	1,022,663
50	-11,000	40,000	132,442	254,826	122,384	1,155,310	1,022,867
51	9,000	20,000	159,459	298,970	139,511	1,202,970	1,043,512
52	9,000	20,000	187,718	338,553	150,834	1,252,494	1,064,776
53	29,000	0	196,358	380,663	184,305	1,303,935	1,107,577
54	29,000	0	205,395	425,465	220,070	1,357,398	1,152,002
55	29,000	0	214,849	473,094	258,245	1,413,030	1,198,181
56	29,000	0	224,737	523,645	298,907	1,470,961	1,246,224
57	29,000	0	235,081	577,341	342,260	1,531,293	1,296,212
58	29,000	0	245,900	634,379	388,479	1,594,106	1,348,205
59	29,000	0	257,218	695,138	437,920	1,659,590	1,402,372
60	29,000	0	269,056	759,831	490,774	1,727,839	1,458,783
61	29,000	0	281,440	828,624	547,184	1,798,976	1,517,537
62	29,000	0	294,393	899,104	604,711	1,872,513	1,578,120
63	29,000	0	307,942	972,906	664,963	1,947,399	1,639,457
64	29,000	0	322,115	1,050,112	727,997	2,023,717	1,701,602
65	29,000	0	336,941	1,130,931	793,990	2,101,555	1,764,614
66	0	0	351,943	1,185,831	833,888	2,146,572	1,794,629
		No Cash In-Flow or Cash Out-Flow Compounding					
67-83		Only While Spending Down the Nest Egg					
84	0	0	734,832	2,682,855	1,948,023	3,326,623	2,591,791
85	-110,373	110,373	880,422	2,802,235	1,921,814	3,425,967	2,545,545
86	-110,373	110,373	1,032,078	2,926,674	1,894,597	3,530,964	2,498,886
Retirement Cash Flow →		110,373	1,190,053	3,056,444	1,866,391	3,642,135	2,452,083
		110,373	1,354,610	3,191,874	1,837,264	3,760,189	2,405,579
89	-110,373	110,373	1,526,024	3,333,430	1,807,406	3,885,796	2,359,772
90	-110,373	110,373	1,704,580	3,478,653	1,774,073	4,016,225	2,311,644
91	-110,373	110,373	1,890,576	3,625,932	1,735,356	4,149,851	2,259,274
92	-110,373	110,373	2,084,322	3,775,303	1,690,981	4,285,588	2,201,266
93	-110,373	110,373	2,286,141	3,926,155	1,640,014	4,422,889	2,136,748
94	-110,373	110,373	2,496,369	4,078,116	1,581,748	4,561,498	2,065,130
95	-110,373	110,373	2,715,356	4,230,774	1,515,418	4,701,330	1,985,974
96	-110,373	110,373	2,943,468	4,383,828	1,440,361	4,842,457	1,898,990
97	-110,373	110,373	3,181,084	4,538,462	1,357,378	4,984,801	1,803,717
98	-110,373	110,373	3,428,601	4,694,383	1,265,782	5,128,399	1,699,798
99	-110,373	110,373	3,686,431	4,851,281	1,164,850	5,273,247	1,586,815
100	-110,373	110,373	3,955,004	5,008,782	1,053,778	5,419,587	1,464,582
101	-110,373	110,373	4,234,768	5,165,962	931,194	5,567,669	1,332,901
102	-110,373	110,373	4,526,189	5,323,891	797,703	5,715,887	1,189,698
103	-110,373	110,373	4,829,752	5,482,501	652,749	5,864,139	1,034,387
104	-110,373	110,373	5,145,963	5,641,711	495,748	6,012,502	866,539
105	-110,373	110,373	5,475,350	5,801,342	325,991	6,160,957	685,606
106	-92,026	92,026	5,799,350	5,961,642	162,291	6,309,617	510,267

This illustration assumes a healthy 35 year old male when the contract is issued.
Hypothetical illustrations should not be used to predict or project investment results.

There is enough collateral capacity in the life insurance policy for accessing $110,373 of loans (against the death benefit) each year from the life insurance company through age 105.

Regarding question #3 - What if the new money was still flowing into the 401(k) plan and you didn't buy the life insurance?

If you continue to fund the 401(k) plan using the same growth assumptions, you would have a $2,900,000 nest egg. This is instead of $2,000,000 without the additional contributions to the 401(k) plan to access at the rate of 4%. The $2,900,000 nest egg would provide a spendable after-tax retirement cash flow of $87,000 per year versus $110,373. This is still 27% short of what your cash flow could be if you owned a life insurance policy and had a smaller nest egg to spend. The following diagram illustrates this scenario:

	$2.9 Million Nest Egg				$2 Million Nest Egg				
Age	Con–serve Gross With–drawal	Con–serve Tax Rate Per–centage	Con–serve Taxes Paid	Con–serve Pur–chasing Power	Con–sume Gross With–drawal	Con–sume Tax Rate Per–centage	Con–sume Taxes Paid	Con–sume Pur–chasing Power	Perc–entage More
65	116,000	25%	-29,000	87,000	147,164	25%	-36,791	110,373	27%
66	116,000	25%	-29,000	87,000	147,164	25%	-36,791	110,373	27%
67	116,000	25%	-29,000	87,000	147,164	25%	-36,791	110,373	27%
68	116,000	25%	-29,000	87,000	147,164	25%	-36,791	110,373	27%
69	116,000	25%	-29,000	87,000	147,164	25%	-36,791	110,373	27%
70	116,000	25%	-29,000	87,000	147,164	25%	-36,791	110,373	27%
71	116,000	25%	-29,000	87,000	147,164	25%	-36,791	110,373	27%
72	116,000	25%	-29,000	87,000	147,164	25%	-36,791	110,373	27%
73	116,000	25%	-29,000	87,000	147,164	25%	-36,791	110,373	27%
74	116,000	25%	-29,000	87,000	147,164	25%	-36,791	110,373	27%
75	116,000	25%	-29,000	87,000	147,164	25%	-36,791	110,373	27%
76	116,000	25%	-29,000	87,000	147,164	25%	-36,791	110,373	27%
77	116,000	25%	-29,000	87,000	147,164	25%	-36,791	110,373	27%
78	116,000	25%	-29,000	87,000	147,164	25%	-36,791	110,373	27%
79	116,000	25%	-29,000	87,000	147,164	25%	-36,791	110,373	27%
80	116,000	25%	-29,000	87,000	147,164	25%	-36,791	110,373	27%
81	116,000	25%	-29,000	87,000	147,164	25%	-36,791	110,373	27%
82	116,000	25%	-29,000	87,000	147,164	25%	-36,791	110,373	27%
83	116,000	25%	-29,000	87,000	147,164	25%	-36,791	110,373	27%
84	116,000	25%	-29,000	87,000	147,164	25%	-36,791	110,373	27%

Regarding question #4 - what if this isn't qualified plan (401(k)) money?

The bottom-line answer to this question is that the after-tax cash flow on the "consume principle" side of the ledger goes up every year because the taxes due each year goes down. That means that the percentage more spendable cash flow each year increases, showing that the advantage of having a permanent life insurance contract is better each year.

Taxes go down on the "consume principle" side because the amount of nest egg earning 4% each year goes down (and taxes stay the same on the "conserve principle" side). If less is earning 4%, less is taxable. This results in less income taxes and more spendable cash flow as long as tax rates stay the same. If tax rates go up, they go up on both sides of the ledger. Having a reducing taxable base mitigates the risk of taxes going up in the future.

Let's look at both sides of the diagram:

Age	Con–serve Gross With–drawal	Con–serve Tax Rate Per–centage	Con–serve Taxes Paid	Con–serve Pur–chasing Power	Con–sume Gross With–drawal	Con–sume Tax Rate Per–centage	Con–sume Taxes Paid	Con–sume Pur–chasing Power	Per–centage More
65	80,000	25%	-20,000	60,000	147,164	25%	-20,000	127,164	112%
66	80,000	25%	-20,000	60,000	147,164	25%	-19,328	127,835	113%
67	80,000	25%	-20,000	60,000	147,164	25%	-18,630	128,534	114%
68	80,000	25%	-20,000	60,000	147,164	25%	-17,903	129,260	115%
69	80,000	25%	-20,000	60,000	147,164	25%	-17,148	130,016	117%
70	80,000	25%	-20,000	60,000	147,164	25%	-16,362	130,801	118%
71	80,000	25%	-20,000	60,000	147,164	25%	-15,545	131,618	119%
72	80,000	25%	-20,000	60,000	147,164	25%	-14,695	132,468	121%
73	80,000	25%	-20,000	60,000	147,164	25%	-13,811	133,352	122%
74	80,000	25%	-20,000	60,000	147,164	25%	-12,892	134,271	124%
75	80,000	25%	-20,000	60,000	147,164	25%	-11,936	135,227	125%
76	80,000	25%	-20,000	60,000	147,164	25%	-10,942	136,221	127%
77	80,000	25%	-20,000	60,000	147,164	25%	-9,908	137,255	129%
78	80,000	25%	-20,000	60,000	147,164	25%	-8,833	138,331	131%
79	80,000	25%	-20,000	60,000	147,164	25%	-7,715	139,449	132%
80	80,000	25%	-20,000	60,000	147,164	25%	-6,551	140,612	134%
81	80,000	25%	-20,000	60,000	147,164	25%	-5,342	141,822	136%
82	80,000	25%	-20,000	60,000	147,164	25%	-4,084	143,080	138%
83	80,000	25%	-20,000	60,000	147,164	25%	-2,776	144,388	141%
84	80,000	25%	-20,000	60,000	147,164	25%	-1,415	145,748	143%

There are a number of things to notice as you compare this diagram with the diagram of the money as qualified plan money (401(k)).

1. The taxes are the same in year 1. That is because each side has the same taxable income if this was after-tax money and not qualified plan money. In an after-tax account (as illustrated here), only the interest is taxable on both sides. In a qualified plan account, both the principle and interest is

taxable because the taxes on the contributions to the 401(k) were postponed until distribution.

2. The taxes begin to go down in year 2 and every year after that. This is because each year you consume principle, there is less principle earning. Consequently, there is less taxable income and, as long as tax rates stay the same, there is less tax to pay.

3. By the year you turn 84-years-old and the last year there is money left in your nest egg; what you are drawing from your nest egg is virtually tax-free.

4. By the year you turn 84, you are now used to a spendable cash flow of $147,164 because you have been paying less tax each year. That means that when you turn to the life insurance contract when you turn 85, we need to plan for distributions of $147,164 and not $110,373 (which was necessary if the nest egg was from a qualified plan). Let's see how long the life insurance contract would last:

END OF YR AGE	NET OUTLAY	LOAN AMOUNT RECEIVED	ENDING LOAN BALANCE	GROSS CASH VALUE	NET CASH VALUE	GROSS DEATH BENEFIT	NET DEATH BENEFIT
46	29,000	0	0	102,180	102,180	979,735	979,735
47	9,000	20,000	20,921	137,097	116,177	1,021,603	1,000,683
48	9,000	20,000	42,804	174,025	131,221	1,064,725	1,021,921
49	-11,000	40,000	86,615	213,224	126,609	1,109,278	1,022,663
50	-11,000	40,000	132,442	254,826	122,384	1,155,310	1,022,867
51	9,000	20,000	159,459	298,970	139,511	1,202,970	1,043,512
52	9,000	20,000	187,718	338,553	150,834	1,252,494	1,064,776
53	29,000	0	196,358	380,663	184,305	1,303,935	1,107,577
54	29,000	0	205,395	425,465	220,070	1,357,398	1,152,002
55	29,000	0	214,849	473,094	258,245	1,413,030	1,198,181
56	29,000	0	224,737	523,645	298,907	1,470,961	1,246,224
57	29,000	0	235,081	577,341	342,260	1,531,293	1,296,212
58	29,000	0	245,900	634,379	388,479	1,594,106	1,348,205
59	29,000	0	257,218	695,138	437,920	1,659,590	1,402,372
60	29,000	0	269,056	759,831	490,774	1,727,839	1,458,783
61	29,000	0	281,440	828,624	547,184	1,798,976	1,517,537
62	29,000	0	294,393	899,104	604,711	1,872,513	1,578,120
63	29,000	0	307,942	972,906	664,963	1,947,399	1,639,457
64	29,000	0	322,115	1,050,112	727,997	2,023,717	1,701,602
65	29,000	0	336,941	1,130,931	793,990	2,101,555	1,764,614
66	0	0	351,943	1,185,831	833,888	2,146,572	1,794,629
No Cash In-Flow or Cash Out-Flow, Compounding Only While Spending Down the Nest							
67-83				Egg			
84	0	0	734,832	2,682,855	1,948,023	3,326,623	2,591,791
85	-147,164	147,164	918,746	2,802,235	1,883,490	3,425,967	2,507,221
86	-147,164	147,164	1,110,322	2,926,674	1,816,352	3,530,964	2,420,641
87	-147,164	147,164	1,309,882	3,056,444	1,746,562	3,642,135	2,332,254
Retirement Cash Flow		147,164	1,517,756	3,191,874	1,674,119	3,760,189	2,242,434
		147,164	1,734,292	3,333,430	1,599,139	3,885,796	2,151,505
90	-147,164	147,164	1,959,850	3,478,653	1,518,803	4,016,225	2,056,375
91	-147,164	147,164	2,194,806	3,625,932	1,431,126	4,149,851	1,955,045
92	-147,164	147,164	2,439,552	3,775,303	1,335,751	4,285,588	1,846,036
93	-147,164	147,164	2,694,496	3,926,155	1,231,659	4,422,889	1,728,394
94	-147,164	147,164	2,960,062	4,078,116	1,118,054	4,561,498	1,601,436
95	-147,164	147,164	3,236,694	4,230,774	994,080	4,701,330	1,464,636
96	-147,164	147,164	3,524,852	4,383,828	858,976	4,842,457	1,317,605
97	-147,164	147,164	3,825,017	4,538,462	713,446	4,984,801	1,159,785
98	-147,164	147,164	4,137,688	4,694,383	556,694	5,128,399	990,711
99	-147,164	147,164	4,463,388	4,851,281	387,894	5,273,247	809,859
100	-147,164	147,164	4,802,658	5,008,782	206,124	5,419,587	616,929
101	-6,660	6,660	5,009,707	5,165,962	156,255	5,567,669	557,963

This illustration assumes a healthy 35 year old male when the contract is issued. Hypothetical illustrations should not be used to predict or project investment results.

Even at this increased level of retirement loan activity against the life insurance contract, the cash flow could continue through age 100.

This example illustrates the impact life insurance has on drawing down a nest egg rather than living on interest only without life insurance. It assumes that during your accumulation stage of life you have achieved the $2,000,000 nest egg.

There are a number of reasons why you may not achieve the $2,000,000 nest egg if you don't use the qualified plan (before tax accumulation). For instance, in this example you may not accumulate $2,000,000 because you need to pay income taxes on the growth of your nest egg during the accumulation years. Turn back to the example of the $2,900,000 vs. $2,000,000 nest eggs. In this example the $2,000,000 still provides 24% more retirement cash flow, than $2,900,000 does accessing interest only. This illustrates that if the nest egg had otherwise been $2,900,000 you could have paid $900,000 in taxes during its accumulation and still would have had more retirement cash flow.

Chapter 13

Uncommon Knowledge

I am often asked why everyone isn't doing this. The answer is that everyone who understands *is* doing this. If you have carefully read and seriously absorbed the financial principles of life insurance uncovered in this book, you now understand as well. You now possess uncommon knowledge.

There is a finite amount of information that humans know about the universe. All of this known information falls into three categories:

First, there is a certain amount of information that you know, and you are aware that you know it. Some examples include: your name, your birth date, and the name of your spouse and your children. There is no doubt that you know it. You might say that you are "consciously competent" of this information.

Second, there is a large amount of information that you are aware that you know nothing about. You know that these things are "out there," but you really don't know anything about them. Some examples might be: nuclear physics, how to perform brain surgery, and the full value of the constant "Pi." You might say that you are "consciously incompetent" of this information.

Finally, all of the rest of the information that is out there represents information that you don't know, and you're not even aware that you don't know it. You are "unconsciously incompetent" in these areas. It doesn't mean that the information doesn't exist; it just means that you are currently unaware of its existence. As a result, this information is currently sitting in your "blind spot." Information in your blind spot is similar to a car in your blind spot. You drive in your car and you look in the rear-view mirror and nothing is there. You then look in the side mirror and still nothing is there. Then, you turn your head 20 degrees over your left shoulder and what you see is a 4,000 pound car traveling at exactly the same rate of speed that you are! It's not that the car just appeared out of nowhere when you turned your head, but it was there the entire time. You just couldn't see it until you viewed it from a new perspective!

Perhaps this book has helped you turn your head 20 degrees and you have discovered something you have never seen before. Nobel Prize winner Albert Szent-Györgyi said, "discovery consists of seeing what everyone else has seen and thinking what nobody has thought."

There are three ways to expand what you know. The first is the experiences you have in the places you go. The second is the personal education you get by the books you read. This is where this book comes in. The final way is by transferring knowledge by talking to the people you meet in life. This is where the financial advisor who gave you this book comes in. If you obtained this book without the referral of a financial advisor, the very best decision you can make is to find an advisor who understands the contents of this book. However, talking with the wrong advisor could be detrimental to your financial health. Let's consider why.

Ask yourself the following questions: how much income do you think it takes to put a combined income household into the top 25% of all income earners in the U.S. today? How much do you think it would take to put somebody in the top 10%? What about the top 5%? The top 1%?

You see, to be in the top 25% it only takes $67,000. The top 10% is $114,000, the top 5% is $160,000 and the top 1% is only $380,000. (Summary of Federal Income Tax Data, 2010 www.taxfoundation.org). Where are you on this scale? So, does that mean your income is relatively common or uncommon? That's right, if you earn $67,000 per year, you possess an uncommon income. Now before I showed you these numbers, would you have said your income was common or uncommon? That's right, most people consider they earn a common income, because everybody you know makes the same kind of money you make. But in reality, the income you make is relatively uncommon because 75% of the population earns less income than you do. If you are just beginning your career, you should ask this question, "*will* my income be common or uncommon as defined above?" Without answering this question, you may discount the principles in this book and believe they do not apply to you. Anyone striving for a better future and serious about wealth accumulation and retirement distribution must take these principles seriously

Consider this as well: the top 1% of income earners pay 38% of all taxes in this country. The top 5% pay 59%, the top 10% pay 70%, and the top 25% pay over 86% of the nation's tax burden. Do you think that advice for common income earners focuses on the principles shared in this book? No, probably not.

So what kind of financial strategies should you be using in your financial world? Should you be doing the same common things that everyone else is doing? Or should you maybe be doing things differently?

The good news is that some of what I "know that I know" is currently sitting in your blind spot. So, by sharing what I know, I hope to help you to expand that which you know.

Addendum

After the first peer review of this book, the comment was made that I ought to conclude the book by illustrating the possibilities of a person who chooses to save the same amount of money as they were paying on their mortgage: $1,500 per month for 30 years. So here is "the rest of the story."

If a healthy 35-year-old saves $1,500 per month for 30 years utilizing a life insurance contract for those savings, their policy could provide almost $240,000 of annual tax-free distributions from age 85 to 100 (if current dividend rates are projected for the life of the life insurance policy). This, of course, assumes that you are able to provide an adequate source of retirement funds between ages 65-84 from your other assets. But that is easier with the life insurance since you can consume both the principle and the interest of those other assets rather than having to live on just the interest only.

END OF YR AGE	NET ANNUALIZED OUTLAY	LOAN AMOUNT RECEIVED	ENDING LOAN BALANCE	GROSS CASH VALUE	NET CASH VALUE	GROSS DEATH BENEFIT	NET DEATH BENEFIT
84	0	0	0	2,951,516	2,951,516	3,741,699	3,741,699
85	-239,745	239,745	250,779	3,097,040	2,846,261	3,862,330	3,611,551
86	-239,745	239,745	513,101	3,249,873	2,736,773	3,991,230	3,478,129
87	-239,745	239,745	787,496	3,410,481	2,622,986	4,129,175	3,341,680
88	-239,745	239,745	1,074,519	3,579,416	2,504,897	4,277,127	3,202,607
89	-239,745	239,745	1,374,754	3,757,445	2,382,691	4,436,099	3,061,346
90	-239,745	239,745	1,688,806	3,941,640	2,252,834	4,602,768	2,913,962
91	-239,745	239,745	2,017,313	4,129,919	2,112,606	4,774,948	2,757,635
92	-239,745	239,745	2,360,939	4,322,171	1,961,232	4,951,132	2,590,193
93	-239,745	239,745	2,720,381	4,517,599	1,797,219	5,130,440	2,410,059
94	-239,745	239,745	3,096,366	4,715,588	1,619,222	5,312,350	2,215,984
95	-239,745	239,745	3,489,656	4,915,666	1,426,010	5,496,634	2,006,978
96	-239,745	239,745	3,901,047	5,117,467	1,216,420	5,683,212	1,782,165
97	-239,745	239,745	4,331,372	5,322,649	991,276	5,871,889	1,540,516
98	-239,745	239,745	4,781,503	5,531,126	749,623	6,062,445	1,280,942
99	-239,745	239,745	5,252,352	5,743,183	490,831	6,254,633	1,002,281
100	-239,745	239,745	5,744,871	5,959,478	214,607	6,448,256	703,385

This illustration assumes a healthy 35 year old male when the contract is issued. Hypothetical illustrations should not be used to predict or project investment results.

Afterthought

Please refer back to the opening page of the book containing the disclosure information. These disclosures are important, and I want to emphasize that your particular situation is different from everyone else. You should be consulting with a qualified life insurance professional who also understands the principles in this book. Attempting to apply these principles without the aid of a qualified life insurance professional would be like trying to drive from Los Angeles to New York City without a roadmap or GPS guidance.

Throughout the book I have made other disclosure statements and qualified some of my writing. These are included because not only is every reader different from each other, but life insurance companies are different from each other as well. When you apply these principles, look for a life insurance company that offers as many of the benefits of life insurance that I have illustrated. Again, the guidance of a qualified life insurance professional will help in choosing the life insurance company you choose to engage in this vital aspect of your financial planning.

About

Bryan S. Bloom, CPA

Bryan began his financial career immediately following earning his CPA credentials and Bachelor's Degree in Accountancy from the University of Illinois. Later he earned his Master's Degree in Business Administration from the University of Illinois Executive MBA program. His career started as a staff accountant for the State Universities Retirement System of Illinois where he eventually became the Chief Financial Officer. After 19 years of experience in public retirement matters, he worked for 5 years with Benefit Planning Consultants, Inc. - a third party administration corporation overseeing private retirement plans. He is currently associated with Chesser Financial, where he has been assisting individuals in their personal retirement planning for the last 13 years.

Bryan earned Million Dollar Round Table membership within four months at Chesser Financial. He earned VIP of the Year award from Ohio National Financial Services that same year. In 2010, Bryan was recognized by Ohio National with their Chairman's Navigator Award, recognizing him for the personal integrity Bryan exhibits with his clients and business relationships.

Bryan and his spouse of 32 years, Pam, live in Champaign, Illinois, and are avid fans of The University of Illinois Fighting Illini. They have two daughters, Callie and Corrie.

You can contact Bryan at bryan@chesserfinancial.com

CPSIA information can be obtained at www.ICGtesting.com
Printed in the USA
LVOW04s1212230715

447351LV00005B/24/P

9 780741 499769